MOON MAGIC

Your Complete Guide to Harnessing the Mystical Energy of the Moon

DIANE AHLQUIST

ADAMS MEDIA
NEW YORK LONDON TORONTO SYDNEY NEW DELHI

Adams Media
An Imprint of Simon & Schuster, Inc.
100 Technology Center Drive
Stoughton, MA 02072

First Adams Media trade paperback edition DECEMBER 2017

ADAMS MEDIA and colophon are trademarks of Simon and Schuster.

For information about special discounts for bulk purchases, please contact Simon & Schuster Special Sales at 1-866-506-1949 or business@simonandschuster.com.

The Simon & Schuster Speakers Bureau can bring authors to your live event. For more information or to book an event contact the Simon & Schuster Speakers Bureau at 1-866-248-3049 or visit our website at www.simonspeakers.com.

Interior design by Colleen Cunningham
Interior illustrations by Claudia Wolf
Interior stars image © 123RF/yewkeo

Manufactured in China

10 9 8 7 6 5 4 3 2 1

Library of Congress Cataloging-in-Publication Data has been applied for.

ISBN 978-1-5072-0501-3
ISBN 978-1-5072-0502-0 (ebook)

Contains material adapted from the following titles published by Adams Media, an Imprint of Simon & Schuster, Inc.: *The Everything® Busy Moms' Cookbook* by Susan Whetzel, copyright © 2013, ISBN 978-1-4405-5925-9; *The Everything® Guide to the MIND Diet* by Christy Ellingsworth and Murdoc Khaleghi, MD, copyright © 2016, ISBN 978-1-4405-9799-2; *The Everything® Easy Mexican Cookbook* by Margaret Kaeter and Linda Larsen, copyright © 2015, ISBN 978-1-4405-8716-0; *The Quick and Easy Vegetarian College Cookbook* by Adams Media, copyright © 2017, ISBN 978-1-5072-0419-1.

"Divination During a Full Moon" in Chapter 13 has been adapted from *The Complete Idiot's Guide to Fortune Telling* by Diane Ahlquist, copyright © 2006 by Diane Ahlquist, ISBN 978-1-59257-539-8.

ACKNOWLEDGMENTS

There are many people I would like to thank who had to do with the writing of this book.

I would like to acknowledge, you, the reader of this book. Whether someone gave it to you, you bought it, or are sitting at a bookstore reading it—thank you. Maybe you received it by mistake when you ordered a quilting book or a how-to-decorate-a-man-cave guide. However it came into your possession, you have it in front of you now. Hence, if you have gotten this far and are one of the few who read acknowledgements…hugs and blessings. I know there is something in here that will add a positive note to your life.

I would also like to thank the following:

Claudia Hilton, who told me at lunch, "How is that working for you?" Made me think. Thanks, Claudia! Kandy Corcoran, for her insights on her favorite lunar sight, when the Moon has a ring around it.

Dee, whose input on the book was immensely helpful, informative, and inspirational.

Thanks, Dotty B., in Sarasota, for your thoughts about the Moon phases and days of the week.

Shelly Hagen, for her contribution to and support of this book. Many blessings on your head.

To everyone at Simon & Schuster and Adams Media who made this book possible—not to mention readable! Especially Eileen Mullan, Laura Daly, Brendan O'Neill, and Chris Duffy.

Adrian, my husband, who, out of the kindness of his heart, sampled all the lunar cocktails and contributed some of his own. Additionally, for his understanding and not complaining about eating lots of submarine sandwiches and frozen potpies during the writing of this book.

Home chefs:

Chris Shake, who is a creative, not to mention great, home chef. To think there is a man out there who actually can peel potatoes, cut onions, and knows the meaning of al dente. What a guy!

David Stahl, for his culinary contribution to my lunar recipe section… Thank you so much!

Janet Osterholt, for not only her recipe but also her insights about lunar gardening. Not to mention the call we received from her one night, saying, "Go outside and look at the Moon. There's a ring around it!" I had to reply, "Ring around the Moon—rain comes soon."

Christine Soderbeck, for her Full Moon Breakfast recipe, which is thought to be a cure for hangovers. My husband had one the next day after sampling all those lunar cocktails!

Lori Frenden, with her beautiful smile and good nature, for passing on one of her favorite Jewish recipes.

Angela Bishop, for that Ginger Beer recipe and process. Cheers and Ciao. Get it? Chow. Ha!

My dear friend Janina, for her culinary expertise and partaking in the lunar meal recipes.

My family: Mudder, Bob, Marie, Johnny, Daniel, and Lori Frenden. But wait, there's more. How can I forget those two guys Joshua Frenden (twelve years) and Ethan Frenden (six years) who provided insights about the Moon that I never would have figured out?

Shane, Myka, Bron, Marco, and Valentina are always so supportive and encouraging. Thank you all.

A special thank you to Boston's Christine H. for informing me that those who celebrate the Chinese Mid-Autumn Festival (Moon Cake Day) typically buy their Moon cakes because they can be very complex to make. Who would have known?

CONTENTS

INTRODUCTION

Do you feel a connection to natural spirituality—a sense of belonging to the universe and everything in it? Just as our ancestors relied on the heavens to inform and predict many aspects of life—navigating, planting, the weather, hunting, personal relationships, and even fertility—we, too, can incorporate the powerful energy of the universe in a positive way in modern-day life. The energy of the Moon in particular has a strong effect on human life. The various lunar phases influence our emotions and well-being in different ways. In *Moon Magic*, you'll learn how to harness that power for manifesting your goals, finding emotional balance, and maintaining physical wellness.

You might say I have a special connection with the Moon. After all, I was named after the Moon Goddess, Diana! Though, I must admit that as a child, I didn't think the nighttime orb in our sky was anything special. As an adult, however, I've become more and more aware of and fascinated by the influence that lunar forces play in our lives.

If we look to the skies, we can connect to our world in ways that we may never have thought of.

With so many electronics around us, we can forget how to interact with nature. Look up at the Moon…not down at a screen! Using the Moon's power begins with understanding its potential. From new Moons, to eclipses, blood Moons, and the Supermoon, there are ample opportunities for the Moon to influence your emotions and thoughts. For example, a new Moon can bring change and new perspectives. Knowing when and how to use that power is key to effecting change in your life.

There are myriad ways you can interact with the Moon, such as:

- **MOON MEDITATIONS:** Meditate according to the phases of the Moon. For example, the waning Moon phase is a time to release, banish, remove, or reduce. If there is something or someone you want less of, this is the time to meditate about it.
- **VISION BOARDS:** If you're creative, try making a vision board during a waxing or full Moon phase, when you're more likely to see your photos and drawings turn into the events, things, and circumstances that you desire.
- **MOON ALTARS:** Let's create a Moon altar with candles, crystals, and anything else with which you want to create a "mood."
- **GARDENING:** Try cultivating a lunar herb garden to satisfy your green thumb and access the Moon's energy. (Did you know that throughout the second week of the lunar cycle, as the Moon is waxing and becomes full, leaf growth is accelerated due to extra exposure to the light of the Moon?)
- **COOKING:** Use the lunar recipes I provide to make meals that are seasonal and lunar friendly. Nothing like fresh shrimp to cool you and your skywatcher friends in the summer. In fact, they look like little waxing Moons, don't they?

You are the captain of your own ship, so navigate using the Moon and see what amazing destinations you can reach!

part

1

the power of moon magic

The universe is made of energy. Different cultures call this energy different things, but the common understanding is that energy is the base of our existence. Our energy can increase or decrease, just like the visible light in the different phases of the Moon. That lunar effect is part of our way of life, whether we know it or not. The phases of the Moon repeat themselves approximately every 29.5 days, starting with a full Moon and continuing until the next full Moon. In this part, you'll learn more about the Moon and how its energy changes in each phase.

CHAPTER 1
PHASES OF THE MOON

Why Does the Moon Seem to Change Shape?

Ever wonder how the Moon shines, glows, and illuminates different amounts of light down on us? Well, the short answer is, it doesn't. The Moon doesn't have its own light. It reflects the light from the Sun, which makes for beautiful lunar views.

The movement of the Moon orbiting around the earth makes the Moon appear as if it is increasing (waxing) or decreasing (waning) in the sky. These changes are what we know as the phases of the Moon. The Moon is not really changing, but the amount of light we see from Earth is. As we journey through this book, I will refer to the phases as waxing (expanding) or waning (lessening).

Every noticeable phase of the Moon has its own special energy and influence. There are technically eight phases of the Moon: four primary phases and four intermediate phases.

THE FOUR PRIMARY PHASES OF THE MOON

1. New Moon (not the same as the dark Moon)
2. Waxing Moon
3. Full Moon
4. Waning Moon

THE INTERMEDIATE PHASES OF THE MOON

The following are the lesser-known phases of the Moon:

1. **WAXING CRESCENT:** After the dark Moon, still in the first quarter of a waning Moon, we see a crescent sliver of the Moon—less than a half Moon.
2. **WANING CRESCENT:** The Moon is less than half illuminated and gets thinner every night, till it becomes a dark Moon, when illumination is completely gone.
3. **WAXING GIBBOUS:** After the waxing crescent and after the first quarter, the Moon's size still appears to be increasing and is more than half full.
4. **WANING GIBBOUS:** After the full Moon's maximum illumination, the light continually decreases. This is also called the third quarter.

In the spirit of simplicity, we will be focusing on the four primary phases. These are the cycles in which you will be able to spin your Moon magic or enhance your meditations. At the end of the primary phase explanations I have added a fifth phase: the dark Moon.

The New Moon

- **WHAT IT LOOKS LIKE:** This is the primary first phase of the Moon and is sometimes identified as the crescent Moon. This is when the tiniest sliver of light appears in the sky. It looks like the right side of the letter *D*, or the right side of a parenthesis.
- **WHAT IT CAN SUPPORT IN YOUR LIFE:** This phase supports the early stages of developing an idea, activity, or planning anything that

promotes betterment in your future. It is a time of new beginnings, a great period to start new relationships of any kind. It is a starting point for exploring new opportunities. Why worry about the opportunities you missed when fresh prospects are coming toward you? You are basically planting seeds of thoughts that will bloom into goals and start to manifest in the near future. So get ready to find that special love, new career, or even that just-right new sofa!

Waxing Moon

- **WHAT IT LOOKS LIKE:** The Moon appears to grow in size during this phase. It is on its journey to a full Moon.
- **WHAT IT CAN SUPPORT IN YOUR LIFE:** At this stage, the Moon is gaining intensity. Therefore, it makes sense that this is a choice time to concentrate on amplifying things you already have, such as relationships you want to take to that next level. Don't forget your bank account. Would that be a good thing to enlarge? Business growth, perhaps? It's a good time to improve all types of communications as well. This is also a phase that promotes healing, which we will talk about later.

Full Moon

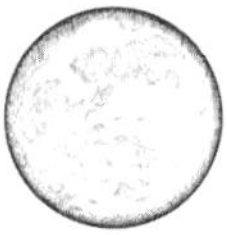

- **WHAT IT LOOKS LIKE:** We all know what the full Moon looks like—a bright, round circle.

- **WHAT IT CAN SUPPORT IN YOUR LIFE:** This is the Moon's most powerful phase. When we see her total illuminated appearance or just know it is there, this is the time of fulfillment. There is much activity around this phase, and it is a time when you should try to perfect thoughts and plans. If you are intuitive or would like to increase your intuition, your psychic abilities may surprise you under this phase. Meditating and manifesting what you want are most intriguing at this time. It's all about strength and controlling vibrations for a better outcome.

Waning Moon

- **WHAT IT LOOKS LIKE:** The Moon now appears as if it is getting smaller and smaller after it was full.
- **WHAT IT CAN SUPPORT IN YOUR LIFE:** This is an occasion for releasing and concluding. Overweight? Start the diet you were planning and maybe you will get smaller and smaller, like the Moon itself during this phase. Get rid of bad habits, difficult relationships, and anything else that is personally toxic, such as negative thinking.

Dark Moon

This is a phase that is not really included among the four main phases, but I have included it for clarity. Although people sometimes will refer to the new Moon and the dark Moon interchangeably, I like to separate the two.

This phase can run from approximately 1.5 to 3.5 days, depending on the positioning of the earth and Sun.

- **WHAT IT LOOKS LIKE:** The dark Moon is when the Moon is not visible. If your calendar shows a dark Moon or a black spot, you can typically figure it occurs not only on that day but also on the day before and after. (Of course, you can always just look up. If you see a sliver of light, you'll know you're seeing the new Moon.)
- **WHAT IT CAN SUPPORT IN YOUR LIFE:** The dark Moon is an occasion for soul searching, thinking, and being by yourself for some alone time. It is a period to dispense with things in your life you don't want or the things you don't want to be a part of.

Keeping Track of the Moon's Phases

To stay organized and maximize the Moon's potential, consider tracking which phase the Moon is in. There are a couple of ways to do that.

With a Calendar

You should invest in a Moon phase calendar, but you can also get the information for free online. Some charts or calendars come in a printable format. Or try an app on your phone (what could be easier?)—some are free, and others, like Deluxe Moon Pro, are just a couple of dollars. An app like Deluxe Moon Pro will not only tell you the phases of the Moon and its exact coordinates in the sky, but it will also tell you which astrological sign the Moon is traveling through on any given day of the year. Take a breeze through your device's app store and see what appeals to you.

Without a Calendar

For those of you who just want to look up, there is an easy way to remember what waning and waxing are. (The full Moon is obvious, as is the dark Moon.) To assist your memory, one way to think about what you're seeing it is to remember the letters DOC for the Northern Hemisphere, which is the half of the earth that lies north of the equator.

When the Moon has a right curve to it, like a D, you're seeing the waxing Moon. It does not need the whole D to be present. Just the right side, or rounded part. The O represents the full Moon. The C is the waning Moon, when the right-hand side of the Moon is not visible.

In the Southern Hemisphere, this is reversed; the letters are COD. The C represents the waxing Moon, and so on. (This would include everyone south of the equator: most of South America, one-third of Africa, all of Antarctica, a tiny part of Asia, portions of Indonesia, and all of Australia/Oceania.)

If you are going to use this "look up" method, rather than the calendar or online reference alternatives, remember that the Moon rises just about 50 minutes later each day. Now you are asking why, right? The reason is because each day the Moon dances a bit, maybe 12–13 degrees to the east, which means the earth has to spin for a slightly longer period of time to bring us around to the location of the Moon in space. (That's the simplified answer. There is a much more scientific explanation available, but let's keep this light reading.)

• • •

The lunar cycle is amazing, and when working with the Moon to create Moon magic, set intentions, or reflect on your life, these phases can help create a new cycle in your life.

CHAPTER 2
ANCIENT BELIEFS ABOUT THE MOON

The Importance of the Moon to Our Ancestors

Ancient civilizations appeared all over the globe: Egyptians, Native Americans, Greeks, Hebrews, Chinese...the list can go on and on. But despite the differences between these cultures and their Moon myths, they all had one thing in common: they recognized the Moon's prominence and power in the night sky, as we do in this modern age.

Each month we have one full Moon. (Okay, sometimes we have *two* full Moons in one month, which is referred to as a blue Moon. We will talk more about a blue Moon in Part Three of this book.) Our ancients had names for everything, so it would make sense that they would have names for the full Moons of each month. Different civilizations labeled the full Moons according to their experiences and what they meant to them and their ancestors. The names were also a means to track or record time and seasons of the year. Sometimes Moon names seem to make a lot of sense in retrospect. But other times there doesn't seem to be any logic behind the names, unless you know the story of how the names came to be.

Ancient civilizations also built legends and lore around the Moon and its phases. Read on to discover some of the more fascinating stories about the Moon.

Native American Full Moons by Month

The Native Americans had different names for their full Moons depending on where they lived. Many full Moons were named for the circumstances of their climate. For example, the Zuni (from southwest New Mexico) called the full Moon in January *dayamcho yachunne*, which translates to "when limbs of trees are broken by snow."

The largest amount of snowfall usually occurs throughout the United States in the month of February. Therefore, the Algonquian tribe called February's full Moon the Hunger Moon because food supplies were scarce at that time of year. The Wishram of Washington and Oregon called it Shoulder to Shoulder Around the Fire Moon. The Kalapuya of the Pacific Northwest called the June Moon "anishnalya," meaning "camas ripe." Camas is a sweet, high-protein root vegatable and food staple. The bulb was fire-baked, tasting akin to a sweet potato or pumpkin.

Today, most of the names of the full Moons that are typically found in publications like the *Old Farmer's Almanac* come from the Algonquin tribes who lived throughout New England and the Great Lakes region.

Here are the names of the full Moons of each month. I have provided their common and lesser-known names.

January

FAMILIAR NAME: Wolf Moon
UNCOMMON NAME: Old Moon or Moon after Yule

Hungry wolves howling can be heard in the coldness of the night air. A time for rejuvenation as a new year begins. A time to get organized and establish new thoughts and take action in a new way, if your old ways weren't working.

February

FAMILIAR NAME: Ice Moon
UNCOMMON NAME: Hunger Moon

Winter's stores are quickly disappearing; this is a time of yearning for new beginnings of the body and the soul.

March

FAMILIAR NAME: Storm Moon
UNCOMMON NAME: Worm Moon

As winter gives way to a thaw, earthworms begin to break the surface in a stage of renewal and rebirth.

April

FAMILIAR NAME: Growing Moon
UNCOMMON NAME: Pink Moon

Spring comes sweeping in with pink wildflowers and new life.

May

FAMILIAR NAME: Hare Moon
UNCOMMON NAME: Milk Moon

Animals are being birthed, bringing forth their mother's milk, a life force in and of itself.

June

FAMILIAR NAME: Mead Moon
UNCOMMON NAME: Dyad Moon

This is the month of Gemini, and the uncommon name of this Moon is a nod to twins (the term *dyad* means "pair") and the sacredness of marriage between god and goddess, the merging of two into one.

July

FAMILIAR NAME: Hay Moon
UNCOMMON NAME: Wort Moon

Wort is another word for herbs, and this is the time when herbs and medicinal plants are gathered and dried in the heat of summer, in preparation for the long winter to come.

August

FAMILIAR NAME: Corn Moon
UNCOMMON NAME: Dispute Moon

Corn is the plentiful harvest this month; it fills our bellies and brings a contentment that allows us to put away our concerns and arguments.

September

FAMILIAR NAME: Harvest Moon
UNCOMMON NAME: Vine Moon

This is the Celtic Moon of elation, all in the name of the hard work needed to complete the harvest, winemaking, and insight for the future.

October

FAMILIAR NAME: Blood Moon
UNCOMMON NAME: Shedding Moon

A time for hunting and also when deer shed their antlers and begin the rut (the period when deer breed) in their drive to sustain and create new life that surpasses the deadness of the winter.

November

FAMILIAR NAME: Snow Moon
UNCOMMON NAME: Tree Moon or Trading Moon

Tree Moon is another Celtic-inspired name. Although it is controversial, some say that the Celts had a tree calendar with each month corresponding to a tree that they believed was sacred. Some call it a lunar tree calendar. Trading Moon refers to the time when the Native Americans would scurry to do last-minute trading before the winter closed in.

December

FAMILIAR NAME: Cold Moon
UNCOMMON NAME: Oak Moon

The oak is the sacred tree of the ancients, solid enough to withstand the harshness of the winter, straddling the old and new years in darkness and light.

Ancient Weather Forecasting

Measuring the seasons and months was not the only thing our ancestors used the Moon for—they also made weather predictions based on how the Moon looked. For example, a halo or circle around the Moon was considered a warning of bad weather to come by many cultures throughout the world. The reason so many believed this was because it seemed to be consistent with the final outcome, which frequently was rain or ill weather. They trusted what they experienced, as did their elders before them. It all seemed to be very valid.

The reality of the matter is that a circle or halo around the Moon happens when tiny ice crystals form within very thin cirrus clouds. The refraction (or splitting) of light off these minuscule ice crystals in the earth's atmosphere cause the circles to appear. That said, high cirrus clouds typically (although not always) are indeed a sign that a storm may be approaching.

A good way to remember this theory is an old saying: "Ring around the moon means rain soon." While looking at that halo, try to count the stars inside it. It is said in Moon lore that the number of stars is an indication of the number of days before the bad weather will arrive. So, the next time you are moongazing and you see a circle, tally up those stars and see how accurate you are.

Oh, and don't forget to carry your umbrella for the next few days.

Using the Moon for Evil

As people and astronomers became more accurate at gleaning celestial information and documented astrological events more thoroughly, some individuals used this knowledge of nature to manipulate others. For example, Christopher Columbus used a lunar eclipse and information he got from an almanac to frighten Jamaican natives into supplying food for his men. He told their group leader that God was upset with the natives because they stopped helping his men and providing food to them. (The natives had stopped helping them only because the natives were being abused and Columbus's sailors were getting greedy.) Columbus explained that God told him he was angry and was going to take the Moon away forever as a way of showing his rage. He also said he would turn the Moon red. After making calculations that took into account his location, Columbus told them when this would take place.

Well, it happened just as he predicted—a lunar eclipse, which made the natives believe the Moon disappeared. The native people were terrified they would never see the Moon again. Shortly before the eclipse was to end, Columbus said God was going to give them another chance if they took care of his men and kept his sailors fed. They did, of course, and when the next Spanish ship arrived, the men were found in good condition, healthy and well fed.

The Moon on Christmas

The Moon phase on Christmas has interesting interpretations in certain cultures. For example:

- In England, it's said that a dark Moon on Christmas night indicates a good harvest for the coming year.
- In the British Isles, a Christmas waxing Moon means just the opposite—the following year's harvest will fall short.
- According to Italian superstitions, if there is a full Moon on Christmas Eve, it is a very good omen for the year ahead, especially for crops or produce. Things will be bountiful.
- Full Moons on Christmas are a rare event in the United States. There have only been eight full Moons that have occurred on the holiday since 1776, the year George Washington crossed the Delaware River under a full Moon in a surprise attack against Hessian forces: 1795, 1806, 1825, 1863, 1901, 1920, 1977, 2015. The next one will be in 2034. To have a full Moon on Christmas implied to religious leaders of colonial New England a very significant period. It was thought to be a natural cleansing of evil thoughts and behaviors in the hearts and minds of parishioners.

- In Ireland, a new/dark Moon on Christmas Eve was considered very blessed and lucky. It signaled a time for innovation and freshness.

The Moon As a Female

The Moon is typically considered a feminine influence by most cultures. She is perceived as strong, powerful, beautiful, luminous, mysterious, and wise. I can certainly understand why so many have assumed she is a female! Another reason for the connection is that the phases of the Moon follow an approximate twenty-eight-day cycle that resembles the average menstruation cycle.

Some ancient cultures believed that the Moon was symbolic of the Triple Goddess, representing the three incarnations of female identity: maiden, mother, and crone.

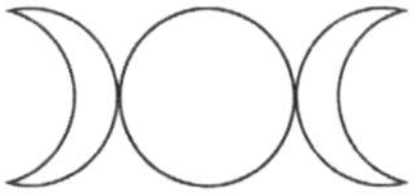

Triple Goddess sign.

- The maiden was associated with the waxing Moon (when the Moon appears to be growing in the sky).
- The full Moon was the mother.
- The waning Moon, which is when the Moon appears to get smaller after the full Moon, was the crone.

The Triple Goddess symbol is also identified with Greek Moon goddesses:

- Artemis was considered the maiden, as she was the virgin goddess of the hunt.

- Selene was associated with the mother, as she was the mother of Endymion's children. (Endymion was not only Selene's lover but also a mortal she fell in love with at first sight.)
- Hecate, the crone, is associated with the night, magic, witchcraft, and guardian of the household. She was wise and influential.

The Moon As Male

Although many cultures have associated the Moon with the feminine, some have thought it to be masculine.

Inuit

One such association comes from the Inuit, who inhabit the Arctic regions of Canada, Alaska, and Greenland and believe in the legend of the Moon God, Anningan.

Anningan's counterpart is his sister, the Sun Goddess Malina. The story goes that the two once resided together and, as siblings are wont to do, got into a quarrel one day. Malina stormed off and Anningan pursued her. Tales differ on the cause of the spat and whether Anningan was following to apologize or to argue some more. But he was so fervent in his pursuit that he neglected to eat and became thinner and thinner, which explains the waning phase of the Moon. Today, the story goes that when the Moon disappears, Anningan has gone away to eat. Then, during the Moon's waxing period, he starts his search for his sister anew. When he finally is able to catch up to Malina, it causes a solar eclipse.

Norse

In Norse mythology the Moon is masculine, and he is named Mani. Mani's sister is Sol, the Sun. Mani soars through the night sky in his horse-drawn chariot, which determines the Moon's waxing and waning. He is pursued by a hateful wolf, and when the wolf gets ahold of Mani, a solar eclipse takes place.

Efik Ibibio

The Efik Ibibio people of Nigeria in West Africa believe that the Sun and the Moon are husband and wife who once lived on the earth. They were one day visited by their friend, Flood, who brought them fish, reptiles, and other relatives. Flood filled their house so high that Sun and Moon had to take refuge on their roof! Flood rose even higher, so Sun and Moon had to leap into the sky.

Luyia

The Luyia people of Kenya in East Africa believe the Sun and Moon were brothers. Moon was the elder, wiser, and stronger sibling, and jealous Sun picked a fight with him. They fought, causing Moon to crash into a pit of mud, dimming his light. God stepped in to stop the fighting, separating the two by ordering Sun to shine during the daytime hours and Moon to take to the night sky.

• • •

Although we live in a scientific world and everyone is eager to see, feel, and touch all the facts, the Moon still carries an irresistible sense of magic, mesmerism, and mystery. Her appearance alone is intriguing, and she changes so often that no matter how much science we have, there just seems to be something more to that bright orb in the night sky. Maybe our ancients, in explaining the patterns and purpose of the Moon, did tap into some things that can never be truly understood.

CHAPTER 3

HOW DOES THE MOON AFFECT US?

The Moon's Effect on Our Planet

The Moon has a powerful influence over many aspects of life here on our big blue planet. The Moon is Earth's constant partner in a cosmic dance, and their relationship is actually credited with the evolution of life on Earth. According to current scientific thought, the Moon has an amazing impact on our planet:

- The gravitational pull of the Moon makes the climate on Earth temperate, with predictable seasons, tolerable temperatures, and moderate winds.
- The Moon stabilizes the tilt of Earth's axis.
- The Moon slows the spin of Earth so we humans can thrive.
- The Moon's lunar cycle powers the tides. This lunar tidal influence helped to create an environment in which the precursors to RNA and DNA flourished.
- The light of the Moon also gives off certain signals that spark the spawning of various marine species. (You'll learn more about this later in the chapter.)

Clearly, the Moon is much more than just something interesting to look at in the sky!

How Specific Moon Phases Can Affect People

The belief that Moon phases are associated with behavior and human consciousness goes back about as far as human history itself. For example, many people remark that they are more accident-prone, erratic, emotional, and/or creative with a full Moon in the sky. Here are some examples of real-life ways that different Moon phases affect everyday people.

Waxing Moon

My shoe-loving hairstylist's feet swell with the waxing of the Moon, and she never finds a shoe sale she can get excited about during that phase. She tells me that when the Moon is waxing, she has to wear her flats because her toes swell so much. The rub is, her "urge" to buy shoes also increases, but she can't because they never fit. What's interesting to me is that she has both a physical Moon effect and a mental Moon effect.

Full Moon

I was talking to a decorator who showed me her portfolio. I noticed there was inconsistency in her results. Some spaces where absolutely beautiful, demonstrating much thought and effort, while others were so-so, resembling something most people could do themselves. I didn't want to be rude and ask her why there was a difference—instead, I asked if she worked with someone else. The answer was no.

She had dates on her project photos that indicated the day she started on each of them. That's when I noticed a pattern: when she started her projects and sketched them out on the days of the full Moon (approximately one day before, the day of, and the day after), they were much more creative. She is not a believer of anything other than logic and facts. I asked her if I could point something out about the phases of the Moon and her projects, and she kindly said, "No, thank you." But I knew.

Some artists have the same creative flows and don't even realize that the Moon has something to do with it. If you completed a creative project, whether it came out good or bad, and kept a record of when you worked on it, check it out and see if this tendency holds true for you. You can learn a lot about yourself.

Waning Moon

I have a friend who has a weight problem, and every time she starts her latest diet on a waxing or full Moon, she doesn't lose a pound. If she starts on a waning Moon, the weight seems to come off quicker. She has lost seventeen pounds in five months by starting her diet when the Moon wanes. The interesting thing is, she did not do this intentionally according to the Moon's phases. She just noted on a calendar when she started to really make efforts and when she didn't try too hard. I was the one who took her calendar to see if there was a correlation, and low and behold, the key to her dieting success was a waning Moon.

Dark (New) Moon

I always research my books in many ways. One of my favorite strategies is to ask people their own experiences when it comes to the information in my books. So yet again, through conversation and a few questions with a friend of a friend at an event, I came across Ashley. Ashley was twenty-eight years old and told me she stopped drinking coffee because it kept her up at night. My question was, "Is that working for you?" Her answer: "Not really. Well, sometimes. No, I don't think so." She said she only sleeps through the night three days a month!

I couldn't resist except to ask her if those three days were in order or just at random. Well, that she was definite about. "Three days in a row." When I asked her if she noticed that these days corresponded to a Moon phase, she said she did not but was sure it was not at a full Moon. I bribed her with the promise of a gift card from her favorite coffee shop if she would mark down on the calendar when she slept more. Five months and one gift card later, I got my answer. It was a dark Moon, when the Moon was not visible in the sky. She just marked days on the calendar and didn't pay attention to

Moon phases. She was only aware of the full Moon because she thought it was beautiful to look at. She had no other interest in the rest of its phases.

So I firmly believe she was telling the truth. I explained and Ashley was happy to know she could drink coffee again, as two or three cups in the morning did not affect her evening sleep.

When this book is completed, I will send her a copy. Maybe she will be a Moon magic enthusiast sometime in the future.

Other Lunar Effects

All of those examples fall under the category of the lunar effect. Recent research confirms what ancients recognized as a result of living close to nature—that a variety of external factors are linked to and regulate the internal rhythms of plant, animal, and human life. It also tells us that not only are many internal rhythms organized and synchronized by external light and dark cues from the environment, but they are also connected to one another, with many being controlled by biochemical (usually hormonal) factors. Seasonal, circalunar, and circadian rhythms are the organizing forces behind all biological functions, including those that facilitate optimal health and regulate sleep, fertility, and reproduction.

For the record: it is doubtful that the lunar effect is strong enough to transform someone from a human into a werewolf during a full Moon.

Sleep Patterns

Although there is no scientific consensus surrounding the effects the Moon has on human sleep patterns, many researchers have found links between the two. Considering the close relationship between the earth and the Moon, it is highly likely that land animals and humans have adapted to the monthly 29.5-day lunar cycle, just as marine organisms have. Circalunar rhythms (our internal clocks) run in concert with several other body systems, including the shorter circadian (daily) patterns that relegate activities like nightly sleep, and the much longer circannual (yearly) rhythms that govern seasonal behaviors in animals, such as hibernation. According to a couple of recent studies published by *Cell Reports* and *Current Biology* in 2013 ("Circadian and Circalunar Clock Interactions in a Marine Annelid" and "Dissociation of Circadian and Circatidal Timekeeping in the Marine Crustacean *Eurydice pulchra*"), multiple biological "timepieces" may help to regulate neural pathways and hormones in many animals. In humans, it's believed that the increased light from a full Moon provides neuronal input to stimulate the sensitive retina, which in turn signals the endocrine cells of the pineal gland to secrete less of the sleep hormone melatonin. This results in extended and increased wakefulness during the full Moon phase.

In the last ten years, scientists have begun to more closely explore connections between Moon cycles and human waking behaviors and sleep patterns. Most sleep research is focused on the full Moon and takes place in carefully controlled conditions, isolating participants from time cues and light sources. While not all evidence points to a clear association, several studies have concluded startling results. One study conducted by researchers at Sweden's University of Gothenburg in 2014 suggests that:

- Sleep is delayed by an average of five minutes and decreased by as much as twenty-five minutes during the full Moon phase!
- Lower levels of melatonin, the sleep hormone, were measured in both adult and child study participants during this phase of the Moon.
- Study members reported sleeping less soundly and changes in sleep patterns were noted by researchers.
- Participants took longer to reach REM sleep and spent 30 percent less time in deep sleep. (This sleep deprivation might account for the clumsiness and erratic behavior some people mention in anecdotal experiences!)

Another investigation studied sleep during the darker nights of the new Moon phase and determined that humans fall asleep more quickly at that time in the lunar cycle.

How Exactly Might the Moon Change Your Sleep Patterns?

These studies imply that the phases of the Moon, most specifically the full Moon, do have a significant effect on sleep, whether or not we sleep in visible moonlight. However, we still do not fully understand the mechanism that controls this function. Here are two areas scientists have considered:

1. **LIGHT:** Scientists tell us the retina of the human eye is very sensitive to blue light reflected from the Moon and that moonlight can affect the mechanism that regulates circadian rhythm, including production of the hormone melatonin. So if we actually slept in direct moonlight, the effects of wakefulness might be even more pronounced.
2. **GRAVITY:** Because humans experience more wakefulness during full Moons—even when we are not directly exposed to moonlight—researchers also considered the idea that gravitational pull might be at work. On this point, scientists seem to agree: the Moon exerts little power on smaller bodies of water (such as the Great Lakes); therefore, the effect on humans (whose water content is miniscule compared to Lake Superior) is very limited and is *not* likely a compelling force.

Sleep and Evolution

Armed with what we know about the circalunar clocks that have developed in other species under the influence of planetary, lunar, and solar cycles, scientists have put forward the idea that somewhere along the line, human bodily systems adapted and now function in a similar fashion.

So what's the evolutionary advantage of less and lighter sleep for humans around the full Moon phase? And what is the external cue that allows our sleep to stay in sync with the Moon? One theory proposed by Malcolm von Schantz, a sleep and circadian researcher at the University of Surrey in the United Kingdom, hypothesizes that the origins of our circalunar clock might be ancient and date back to the emergence of mammals. When asked to comment on the results of a sleep study from the University of Basel in Switzerland for a July 2013 *National Geographic* article by Ker Than, von Schantz reminds us that "mammals evolved through what is called the nocturnal bottleneck. When dinosaurs roamed the earth by day, the night represented a window of opportunity for a new group of vertebrates to evolve." Therefore, we can deduce that:

- Since the evidence tells us that hominoids (ape-like creatures) hunted, thrived, and evolved on the banks of water bodies, they would have been more active during a full Moon, when the gravitational pull on water is strongest, tides vary, and aquatic prey are on the move, mating, and generally more accessible and vulnerable.
- The light of the full Moon would have allowed the predatory hominoids to hunt longer and later into the night.
- Extended and increased wakefulness during a full Moon would also have enhanced their alert response, helping them avoid or evade predators.
- There might have been a circalunar rhythm that synchronized reproductive behaviors in our ancestors, as it still does for some modern marine and land animals today.

With or without the scientific evidence, it's obvious that humans and our sleep patterns are inextricably and deeply connected with planetary and cosmic cycles. If humans didn't respond to the effects of these heavenly solar and lunar bodies, we would be one of very few organisms on Earth that didn't, and it would have been impossible for humans to evolve to the level of complexity that we have attained.

How to Improve Your Sleep

What insights can we glean from this information to help us thrive in the digital days we now live in? If you're having problems sleeping, check the Moon phase on your lunar calendar. If it's a full Moon, you may want to use that extra waking time to do something creative—write a song, dance, or journal. If it's not a full Moon and you or your children are having frequent trouble sleeping, consider that your circalunar clock may be out of sync. Reset your circalunar rhythm by minimizing artificial light in your environment from electronic devices such as TVs, computers, and cell phones in the evening. In other words, make your sleeping environment as dark as a night without the Moon in sight.

Fertility

Fertility is another area of human life that might be affected by lunar cycles. When an animal's internal systems are synchronized with the external rhythms of the universe, organisms are more likely to experience better health, increased fertility, and more successful reproduction. This makes sense, because the biology and behaviors all organisms use to survive is based on their ancestors' ability to successfully exploit, adapt to, and reproduce in a unique environmental ecosystem. In order for our human ancestors to survive, they needed to be aware of and make the most of the dynamic environmental resources at their disposal over the course of their lifetime. The fact that reproductive cycles would synchronize with times that were most advantageous for successful maturation, mating, reproduction, and survival for each species is only natural. Exploring lunar phases and how the Moon affects human fertility and reproduction helps us understand how we can align with and tap into external forces, such as Moon phases, that enhance our well-being.

Melatonin and Fertility

We talked a little bit about melatonin in the section on Moon phases and sleep. Melatonin is a hormone that is secreted by the pineal gland in the brain; its production is naturally regulated by your body, based on exposure to light and dark. (When you are constantly exposed to light, production of melatonin naturally drops.) Its job is to regulate the production and use of other hormones and maintain the circadian rhythm. And as you probably already know, it plays a critical role in the quality of your sleep.

You might not know that melatonin is also intricately related to the reproductive system in both males and females:

- **WOMEN:** In women, it regulates the frequency and duration of the menstrual cycle, when a woman starts (menarche) and stops (menopause) menstruating, implantation and maintenance of a pregnancy, and fetal development. A recent study from the University of Texas Health Science Center at San Antonio suggests that healthy melatonin levels are crucial to fertility. It found that melatonin facilitates healthy egg and sperm production, which are the first steps to conception and a successful pregnancy. It does this by acting as an antioxidant in the ovaries, removing free radicals and preventing cellular damage to eggs.
- **MEN:** In men, melatonin levels are believed to play an essential role in sperm formation, quality, and motility. Several studies have found a direct correlation between low melatonin and male infertility, as well as decreased sperm motility.

Fertility and the New Moon

The fact that women's menstrual cycles typically recur on a regular twenty-eight-day pattern that closely aligns with the 29.5-day lunar cycle hardly seems like a coincidence. We also know that the retina of the human eye is very sensitive to blue light reflected from the Moon and that moonlight can affect circadian rhythm, including melatonin production. Exposure to more light at night, such as during the full Moon phase, lowers melatonin production levels, while the darker phases of the Moon (such as the new Moon) raise melatonin levels.

Knowing that higher levels of melatonin naturally occur at the new Moon and mean healthier sperm and eggs, it should come as no surprise that the new Moon phase is typically the most fertile time for conception to occur. Additionally, according to Professor Charles Kingsland, of the Hewitt Fertility Centre at Liverpool Women's Hospital, the lack of light and cover of darkness would have shielded amorous caveman couples from hungry predators.

In today's modern world of artificial light and blue-lit screens, where we're constantly staying up late watching TV and working on computers, we are constantly exposed to what our bodies consider a supercharged full Moon; subsequently, melatonin levels are running low, wreaking havoc on sleep and fertility. Reclaiming a connection with the rhythm of the Moon and getting eight hours of sleep in total darkness every night at roughly the same time is the first step in supporting healthy circadian and circalunar rhythms. These habits, in turn, can facilitate optimal melatonin production levels and enhance fertility.

A Calm Mind

Some people deal with constant anxiety or have regular panic attacks —maybe due to their job, family, finances, health issues, or environment. Whatever the reason, anxiety is not an ideal state of mind. But is there a way that the Moon can actually make you calm?

The answer is yes. It's a dark Moon—not to be confused with a new Moon. Some people refer to these as one in the same, but there is a slight difference. A dark Moon is when the illuminated side of the Moon is not visible and lasts about two to three days. You can't see the Moon at all with the naked eye during this time. Hence, it is said the energy of the Moon is low and many (though not all) people are calmer.

People do not pay as much attention to this phase of the Moon as they do to a full Moon. Chances are you've heard someone say, "Everyone is acting crazy right now—it must be a full Moon!" But have you ever heard anyone saying, "All the nice people are out today, must be a dark Moon"? Or, "Everyone is acting so well-adjusted, it must be the Moon"?

You might want to carry out your own trial test on this one, as there are few statistics regarding people being more peaceful and laid-back on the night of a dark Moon.

The Lunar Effect on Animals

If the Moon impacts human life in so many ways, clearly it also affects other creatures on the earth, right?

Wolves and Coyotes

Many years ago, I was doing research for an article about wolves and prairie wolves (coyotes). I was going to write about how and why the wolves howl at the full Moon. (Information on the computer was not as plentiful as it is today. "Googling it" had not yet been invented.)

I researched and researched and came to the conclusion that—surprise!—these animals don't actually howl at the Moon. In reality:

- The increased activity of wolves during the full Moon stems from the fact that they can see their prey better as a result of the increased moonlight, causing them to communicate with their fellow wolves more often and more loudly during this time.
- Pictures and drawings of wolves with their faces pointing up to the heavens show how they are projecting their calls so the sound can carry farther.
- More pictures are taken of these nocturnal characters during this time because photographers can see them better; hence, people made an incorrect association between the howling behavior and the full Moon.

Well, my article never got written since it did not make sense to put something out there if there was a logical explanation to the contrary. In spite of that, I still wanted to know: *are* animals affected by the Moon? If it's the lunar light that allows animals such as the wolves to be more productive in their hunting and louder in their communication to others, then the Moon *does* actually influence their behavior.

You can see how the controversy can get puzzling.

Marine Life

I live in Florida, so I am surrounded by not only water but also lots of people who fish, both professionals and weekend anglers. While talking to a fisherman, I mentioned the effects of the Moon on human and animal behavior. I assumed he would be skeptical about the Moon affecting our behavior, but he said he plans his fishing according to the phases of the Moon. Apparently this concept has been utilized for ages. (How would I have known? I simply hunt for fish during any phase of the Moon, at any time of day, at the grocery store.)

So, are fish really affected by Moon phases or is it just a matter of the light again? I've learned through my inquiries and by interviewing the local fishing crowd that many anglers feel that dawn and dusk are the best times for casting a line. However, there are those who stick with moonrise and moonset. These are people who take their fishing very seriously, keeping calendars, tide charts, and anything else that will help them haul in a big catch.

Records from fisherman who use the Moon phases show that the best fishing takes place in the four days preceding the full Moon, which is a waxing Moon, and the four days after the new or dark Moon, which is the phase when the Moon is not visible. The most common theories as to why these phases are peak for fishing have to do with the Moon's effect on tides and currents.

Some say bottom-dwelling fish are more active during these phases because the current stirs them up.

If you like to fish, try the four days before a full Moon and four days after theory. Let nature be your coach.

Vampire Bats

The idea that lunar radiance delights animals is not 100 percent true. Some animals don't like it at all. Take the vampire bat, for instance: they have a tendency to lessen their activity when the Moon is waxing or full. They have many nocturnal predators, and the more visible they are, the better chance they have of becoming some other creature's Moon meal!

Cats and Dogs

Whether animals react to the glow of the full Moon or to some mystical Moon sense, animal activity is most definitely affected by lunar light—or the lack of it. It has been documented that dogs and cats are in animal emergency wards more often when the Moon is waxing or full. Why? Because they can see better, they tend to get into more mischief! So remember to watch your feline and canine friends when the Moon shines bright.

• • •

The belief that Moon phases are associated with behavior and human consciousness is part of our history. In this day and age, many people disregard these legends and myths. All the same there are still plenty of folks who, through their experiences and encounters, will tell you their emotions and psyches are indeed affected by the Moon.

CHAPTER 4
ENERGY BASICS

Different Types of Energy

Modern science teaches us that every part of the universe has energy of some kind. The universe includes so many different types of energy—we often talk about solar energy, electrical energy, chemical energy, and biomass (organic byproduct) energy. But what about lunar energy? We don't hear that too often, but the Moon does, in fact, have energy as well. Most of us recognize that the gravitational pull of the Moon and the Sun cause the rise and fall of sea levels on a daily basis. But this energy also impacts human life and the planet's ability to support other types of living thing. Humans carry energy as well. Our personal energy increases and decreases at different times for a variety of reasons. For example, you might lose energy from not eating properly. Or you might get excited about an unexpected burst of positivity in your life and notice some extra oomph in your energy levels. We have all gone from being in high spirits to down in the dumps and vice versa.

Energy can be contagious too. How many times have you heard it's better to be around positive people than those who are always complaining and have tales of woe? Of course we all need to vent on occasion to special people, or even to strangers. But there is venting...and then there is the perpetual "poor me" syndrome. Our own energy can absorb others', or we can also project our fun spirit onto others.

I have heard it expressed that human energy can be divided into two counterparts: stamina and fatigue. I like that terminology because it is so simple and so true. Despite our best efforts, our stream of liveliness can go from stamina to fatigue, thereby becoming depleted. In those times, it's a good idea to pay attention to why your energy changed and what you can do to rebalance it.

Chi

Balance is a key part of the Chinese views on personal energy. They believe in a universal life force or energy that they call "Chi." There are also other cultures that recognize Chi energy but call it by a different name. Some of these are: Ki (Japanese), Prana (Sanskrit), and Ruach (Hebrew). These traditions all have slightly different perceptions of exactly how energy works. However, they are in agreement that energy is inherent in all things. Many people interpret Chi as not only energy but also air, wind, or vital essences. It has a presence in everyone and everything, even though we cannot see it. When it flows too fast, it is dispersed, and the result is a lack of Chi. When it flows too slowly, the result is stagnation. A steady Chi energy flow in your body is the ideal scenario. People all over the world focus on the state of their Chi for the purpose of creating better health and well-being.

Managing Your Chi

The Chinese believe that keeping your Chi balanced is the way to health and well-being. Here are some ways to do that:

- Meditate (see the Moon-specific meditations in Part 3 for some ideas).
- Practice yoga to help unblock stagnant Chi.
- Take a walk in a nice environment.
- Employ breathing techniques and exercise routines.

A one-time stroll through the park does not a balanced body, mind, and spirit make! Form daily habits that encourage you to relax amidst frequent stressors like work and family responsibilities.

De-Stress

Putting less stress on yourself can balance your Chi. Everyone knows that as simple as it sounds, de-stressing is difficult to do when you have a busy lifestyle. Here is a step-by-step way to reduce stress in your life.

1. Make a commitment to de-stress. Know that you will have to reprioritize certain things in your life, but you can control what gets your attention.
2. Have a specific plan. Write down what bothers you and how you are going to take steps in the future to change those things, such as:
   1. Pay attention to what produces nervousness or worry in your life. If it's your job, develop a short-term strategy for calming yourself until you can move on to another job that suits you better and makes you feel happier.
   2. Get up an hour earlier in the morning so you can achieve goals for that day—getting exercise, paying bills, or responding to emails.

These simple approaches can shift your energy. Even if your life doesn't change in one day, you have made an effort to do something about it. Keep in mind that there are more advanced ways to unblock your Chi, such as hiring a professional who does energy work or studying the subject in depth. A quality organization is the Taoist Tai Chi Society of the USA (www.taoist.org/usa/).

The Moon's Energy

The Moon's energy is more organized and predictable than humans' because each month it repeats itself on a schedule—and it doesn't have to deal with daily emotions and acting and reacting to circumstances. Working with the Moon's energy force can make things flow so much better in your life. For example, you could say, "I want to plan that party for a day when the Moon is waxing, because I know my energy will be great and most of the guests will be in an upbeat mood." Or, on the other hand, you could think, "That's not a good day for that get-together because the waning Moon or dark Moon might make some individuals uninterested and just so-so about the event. And just so-so makes a boring occasion."

Auras

Another ancient belief that surrounds the subject of energy is an aura. The word *aura* comes from the Greek language and means "breath" or "air." It is an invisible emanation; a colorful, multilayered oval of sorts. It arises from and surrounds every person and living thing. Each color, although subtle, signifies a different vibration, which has different meanings. (More on the colors in a minute.)

Seeing Auras

You can actually "see" or "read" your own aura (or someone else's). It an easy process:

1. Choose a quiet time of day and a place where you have privacy and no spectators.
2. You will need a white background and a mirror. If you have a wall mirror already hanging up, you can hang or drape a white sheet behind you, unless the wall behind you is already white. If you have to use a smaller mirror, position it so you have a white wall behind you or in a spot where you can hang a sheet.

3. Stand about three or four feet away and face the mirror. You do not need to see your entire body. The upper part of your body, including your shoulders and your head, will be fine.
4. Stare at the middle of your forehead (your third eye, as some cultures call it).

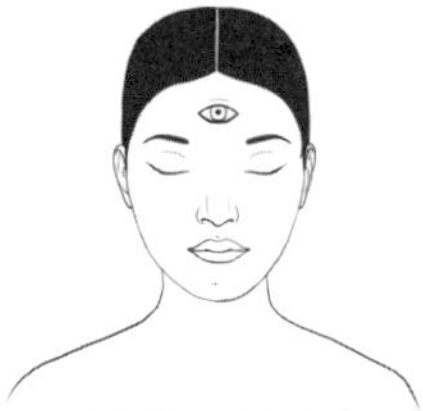

Third eye.

5. Focus on that spot on your head for approximately thirty seconds. Then examine the area with your peripheral vision. All the while, keep your focus on the spot in the middle of your forehead. Continue to concentrate and you will eventually start to see the background become brighter and more in focus. This is your aura.
6. At first you may see just one or two colors; some will see many colors. Usually a person has one or two colors that dominate her aura. Ordinarily, the brighter and more vivid the colors, the healthier or more spiritually evolved you are. The uniformity of the aura also tells you how balanced you are.

Specific Colors

Here are the basic colors and their meanings to give you some context when you see your aura or someone else's.

- **WHITE.** When speaking of white, which is a combination of colors, remember that we're referring to light, not pigment. White (bright light) will always have a positive vibration. We should strive for bright light, not the color white. This light is associated with truth, purity, cleansing, healing, and protection. It further indicates a high level of spiritual attainment and a disposition to help others.

- **RED.** Represents the physical body and can indicate force and stamina. This color can be representative of a person who is self-centered, money-oriented, athletic, or sexual. Deeper shades of red support the negative interpretations, while light shades suggest the more positive interpretations.
- **ORANGE.** Attention to detail, self-control, and optimism. As the Sun can be uplifting, so can people projecting this hue. Some challenges the color implies include trust issues with others—for example, falling in love with people who do not respond as you desire.
- **YELLOW.** If the yellow is pale, it could indicate you are shy and maybe trying to attempt to start a chapter of your life over again with a different approach. A golden yellow implies you have deep inner wisdom and a general sense of well-being. The basic color of yellow shows you have a natural flow of things and enjoy life for the most part.
- **GREEN.** This is the color of nature. You are a good listener and enjoy focusing on healing yourself and others. This is the color of different types of healers. If you see a yellowish shade of green, it can mean uncertainty and even dishonesty.
- **BLUE.** This is the color of truth, meditation, and spirit. Any shade of blue is good. Those who are artistic tend to have a lot of blue in their aura. Blue can also indicate healing and the ability to heal. On occasion, people with blue in their aura can become melancholy or get the "blues," but for the most part, they follow through with projects and are spiritually focused.
- **PURPLE.** This is the mystical color. People with purple in their auras are intuitive and spiritual individuals. This color does not tend to linger too long and will eventually become a deep shade of blue. If it does appear, it means you are having strong insights at the time.

- **BLACK.** This is technically the absence of color and not a color at all. Regardless, for the purpose of interpretation we will list it here. The qualities of black can be good and not so good. In fact, it can confuse you. It may indicate depression, evil, and ill health. On the other hand, it can mean you have a protective shield around yourself—that for the moment, you are in a protective state.

The meanings of the aura colors provided here consist of just the basics. Your aura will change depending on your unique circumstances and experiences. A fun experiment is to try this technique on different phases of the Moon to see how your aura changes. Write down the results so you don't forget and then compare.

Make the Moon's Energy Work for You

The Moon and her many faces and dispositions affects the flow of energy in our bodies. Your life force is forever moving and shifting, even if you can't see it. Therefore, let the Moon do the work and make your journey through life a little easier. I am all for anything that causes less stress and more joy in life. I don't think we are on this planet to see how much negativity we can endure. If we work with nature, the trip is much improved, to say the least.

We should all have goals, and getting from point A to point B doesn't always have to be an immense challenge. There are a few ways to achieve your goals. You can plan your destination...but if you start without a route in mind and the right timing, the train may leave the station while you're still buying your ticket. You'll either have to jump on and spend the ride holding on to the railing of the outside door, or you can try to plan, set your timing up properly, and ride in the dining car with velvet curtains and a scenic view. Either way, you will get to your destination, but I prefer the dining car, personally.

The energy of the Moon can also set a mood. The Moon can make you feel daring, romantic, anxious, sluggish, or scholarly, depending on what phase it's in. With all that influence, lean into it, not away from it. At the very least, be aware of its capacity.

• • •

As we move through this book, you will learn the various ways that lunar energy affects your personal energy—and what's more, you will learn how to work with the various phases of the Moon (each of which have a different influence) to maximize your planning and potential! Like you, the Moon has a life force, and that force affects what happens here on our planet, including within our own bodies. And if you learn to harness it, you can work with the Moon to reach your highest goals and deepest desires.

part

2

harnessing the positive energy of the moon

The Moon releases powerful energy all the time, but each lunar phase has its own energetic frequency that can help you achieve your goals. Knowing which particular frequency is conducive to what you want to undertake is the key to harnessing that energy. The Moon's shifting flow of intensity can empower you to be more creative, balanced, successful, healthy, and happy!

Calculating how and when to use this Moon magic is the springboard to your accomplishments. One of the key secrets is having a sense of when to proceed and when to yield. Even if you have to practice a tad to find out what techniques work best for you, it's worth it. Nature is offering you a shortcut toward victory. Be prepared and use it.

CHAPTER 5

WHEN TO PRACTICE MOON MAGIC

Moon Phases + Days of the Week = A Powerful Combination!

The phases of the Moon (which were discussed in Chapter 1) are key to learning to use the Moon's power for your specific intentions. But you can even learn to take this power a step further by doing your Moon magic on a certain day of the week. By combining a Moon phase with the energy associated with a particular day of the week, you're boosting your intention and opening up even more possibilities!

Here's an added tip: if you decide to combine a Moon phase and a day of the week together, make a little note of what day it was when you did your meditation, spell, or recipe so you can go back later and see how well things worked out. You might just want to tweak things the next time around.

The Days of the Week

Whether you are doing a Moon meditation or just want to be in sync with what the day has to offer, consider the energies associated with each day. Will your intentions and meditations work on other days of the week? Of course they will—but because certain energies are associated with specific days of the week, you might get what you're after faster if you are working with these guidelines instead of working independently of them.

Keep the following days in mind when you are planning on doing any kind of Moon magic, be it planting, meditating, cooking, or spiritual and healing work. Working with the Moon will make things flow better.

Sunday: Associated with the Sun

Sunday is a time to focus on matters that deal with goals, wellness, and merriment. These include personal finances, career advancements, produce or crops, legal matters, "guy stuff," business and professional partnerships, mental and physical health, civic undertakings, and entertainment. This might be a great day to give thought to whether you want to further your education or how to invest wisely.

Monday: Associated with the Moon

Mondays correspond well to things that stereotypically deal with women, family, and the home, such as gardening, cooking, healing, medicine, and beauty. It's also a good day to focus on developing your intuition, past-life regressions, wisdom, and spiritual growth. If you are going to meditate on pursuing a job in the culinary field, this is a great day for that! Plan a trip or look for those antiques you must have. Divination is done well on this day. So get out those tarot cards while you're waiting for your beef stew to heat up and serve it on those vintage plates you just bought at the antique fair!

Tuesday: Associated with Mars

Tuesday relates to things of a physical nature, like getting in shape and physical endurance —activities that are stereotypically more masculine in nature. It also corresponds to anything passionate or sexual. It's a time for new beginnings. If you wanted to meditate on starting a new job in the great outdoors, this would be a good day of the week to do that. Some see

Tuesday as an excellent time to have surgeries or tests. Protection rituals or endeavors are more powerful on this day. Anything involving the military or law enforcement is also enhanced on Tuesday.

Because it is a time for initiating things, for example, this is a good time to think about adopting a pet.

Some people adopt animals via their horoscope sign to see if they will be compatible with their newfound friend. If you are interested in starting a pet adoption process based on your horoscope, you might look into talking to an astrologer you know or find one online, like Magdalena Young at www.12soulsteps.com.

Wednesday: Associated with Mercury

Wednesday is the best time to concentrate on matters that have to do with arts. Communication is another area to focus on today. Make those phone calls or send those emails you were procrastinating about. Consider issues involving contracts, accounting, education, and family members. It's time to hire someone to finally help you with your business. This day also lends itself well to reading books like *Moon Magic* or taking that new astrology class. If you are the artsy-fartsy kind of guy or gal, this is the day for you to think outside the box and get even more creative. Education, memorizing, and visiting friends are associated with this day. Because Wednesday is midweek, it makes us stop and think about whether we are going backward or forward, taking care of ourselves or not, as at this point we can go either way. Therefore, healing is also associated with this day (i.e., do we continue on as in the past or start the restoration of ourselves now?).

Thursday: Associated with Jupiter

Thursday is the best for socializing, traveling long distances, gambling, religious pursuits, and anything related to foreign interests. This is a day of luck, achievement, and self-improvement. Meetings with doctors, lawyers, psychologists, and counselors are good to schedule on Thursdays, as Thursday's energy allows us to develop mentally and spiritually.

Sports competitions and research are good to do on Thursdays. Since the workweek influence is winding down, so is the urgency to get things concluded—such as political resolutions, which some of you may be interested in. Have you been thinking about attending that peaceful rally or telling your local political figures about that new dog park the community needs? If it takes place on a Thursday, give it a whirl. If it does not take place on a Thursday, at least plan for it the Thursday before the event.

Wealth and money matters reign. If you are hoping to get an award or reward, it's a good day to include that intention in meditations.

Friday: Associated with Venus

Friday is ruled by Venus, the planet of love. This is the best time to focus your meditation on romance, love, friendships, dating, pleasure, partners, unions, and fertility. As on Wednesday, which is a day of expression, you can also look into artistic endeavors on Friday, which is not only ruled by the planet of love but also creativity. Social activities and partying are associated with Friday's energy too, of course!

This is an ideal day to engage in anything involving music, fashion, entertaining others, or design. It's a time of healing your body and your mind. Friday is twofold. You can have fun, relax, or do both. Having fun and relaxing is all-healing. Hence, if you need a little mental healing from a stressful week or situation, the vibration of Venus on Friday will be very beneficial. Anything you are passionate about should be in focus on Friday. Don't be embarrassed to be passionate about money, magic, or material things. Friday will suit you whether you want to sit a spell or cast a spell. And keep in mind that when I say "spellcasting," I'm also talking about meditation. (Spellcasting is simply a type of concentration and intention—where you're focusing most of your energy.)

Saturday: Associated with Saturn

Saturday will give you a boost if you need to banish something. It is associated with death but not necessarily physical death—it could be the death of something you want gone, or the end of something that serves no purpose in your life. (This could be a someone too.) Finances and real estate transactions can be in the spotlight on Saturday as well. Other things to include in your meditations are matters that you want to dismiss or that require protection from people, places, or things. Also transformation and spiritual cleansing. So sweep away that negativity from you mind!

Combining Day and Moon Energies

Now that you know the energies associated with the days of the week, and you also know the phases of the Moon, you are ready to put together a strategy for practicing Moon magic that's geared toward achieving a specific goal. However, there are times where you might want to work in reverse—for instance, see what day and Moon phase you're in now, and then see what you could accomplish.

Moon Phases

A quick reminder of the Moon phases and their significance.

- **NEW MOON:** That first gleam of light in a crescent. Focus on new beginnings and starting or preparing for what you want in life.
- **WAXING MOON:** The Moon looks like it is increasing in size. Focus on making things you want to grow come to fruition—from relationships to better health to your financial portfolio.
- **FULL MOON:** When the Moon is at its brightest and looks completely round in the sky. This is a time for increasing your intuition, rituals that require lots of extra energy, or meditations that require very strong concentration.
- **WANING MOON:** The Moon is getting slighter to the eye and so can things you don't want in your life. It's a time to discard of the unwanted in your body, mind, and spirit.

- **DARK MOON:** When the Moon is not visible at all. It's a phase when you may find you need a relaxing retreat—or you just need to retreat to get away from everyone!

Sample Ways to Combine Days and Moon Phases

It's fun and interesting to try to determine which day is the best for achieving specific goals that will help you realize balance in your life. If you have to choose between working in conjunction with a day of the week or a specific Moon phase, the phase will most likely be more powerful. Also, pairing days of the week with optimal Moon phases may seem like it requires an awful lot of organization and planning as you first learn about these powerful energies, but don't forget that combining the two will give you an added edge for better and faster results.

Waxing Moon and Wednesday

Let's say today the Moon is waxing and it is Wednesday. What Moon meditation or rite is best for today?

Remember, waxing means growing, so you should focus on something you want more of or something you want to establish. Now let's look at the day of the week a little more closely. We know that Wednesday has a vibration for communication, so perhaps one of the things you want to accomplish is calling, writing, or emailing potential employers about a job. The forces of establishing communication are aligned for you on this day and in this Moon phase!

Waxing Moon and Thursday

If you really need to communicate an idea or pitch yourself, Thursday is strong with energy that brings luck and good fortune. Dare I say a waxing Moon on a Thursday is a good day to gamble or buy a lottery ticket? Now, I am talking a dollar or two. You do not want to develop a gambling compulsion every Thursday! (The Moon is *not* encouraging you to do that!) But throwing down a few bucks for a scratch ticket after meditating or setting your intention during the correct phase of a Thursday Moon might just pay off big-time!

Waxing Moon and Friday

How about Friday? Well, it's a good day for conjuring up love. So if you find yourself lonely and the Moon is waxing on a Friday, set your intention, and set it strongly. By the following weekend, you might just have a special someone to sing a love song with—or two!

Waning Moon and Saturday

Now, when the Moon is waning, you can work on different intentions. Look to a Saturday if you want to get rid of those guests who have over-stayed their welcome by however many days (you stopped counting at day three—the point at which houseguests and fish begin to stink). Incorporate into your Moon meditation or spell a few minimal sentences aimed directly at the source. You might want to tell your friend it's been so lovely having her, and you can't believe how quickly the time has passed and her visit come to an end! The Moon can help guide you to find just the right words and the right energy to pass this intention along painlessly and subtly. Let the Moon infuse you with gratitude for the visit and graciousness to show your guests the door in the nicest way possible.

If you are forced to evict a tenant, they will most likely go easily after your Moon meditation if you focus on seeing them leaving peacefully with all money you are owed paid in full. So, think Saturday to get rid of things or people in your life you want to remove either temporarily or forever. Saturday is also a good day for banishing or evicting negative energies.

Full Moon Celebrations

Moon magic isn't just about doing meditations on certain days of the week. You can also pour that energy into celebrations. Most moongazers seem to lean toward full Moon celebrations, which can be a time of very strong lunar vibration. In fact, the lunar energy is so strong that it can sometimes throw us a curve if we don't plan ahead.

The full Moon is a great time to commemorate an anniversary, making a commitment to someone, starting a business, or buying your first house. Unfortunately, we can't always celebrate things on the very date they occurred in the past, but we still want to mark the occasion. So, spin some party-planning magic during the full Moon of any month. (You could also hold these types of events during a waxing Moon, but the full Moon also represents excitement and memorable times due to the visual impact of something so majestic. Plus, if it's outside, you can see the food and beverage table better!) You might be celebrating a teenager maturing into an adult or the freedom associated with being newly divorced. It can be a nod to shedding 25 pounds and feeling that a new you is on the horizon. It could be anything that represents a new stage of life after being in a stagnant situation for a long time. It's moving up a spiritual or physical ladder. The full Moon is also tied to our intuition, and it is said that our psychic abilities are at their peak at this phase, so what better time to celebrate!

Meditations and Rituals During Full Moons

All your senses are heightened at the time of a full Moon, which makes it an exceptional time for meditations of any kind, as well as ceremonies or rituals. Your energy is more intense and your natural psychic abilities reach their peak at this time because of the thin veil of energy between the spirit world, the universal life force, and the physical world. In other words, a full Moon puts a lot of psychic energy out there that comes from many different sources. It could be from spirits who have passed on or from your next-door neighbor who just happens to be angry during the full Moon.

Absorbing Energy

When thinking about the energy around you, it's important to remember that you can absorb energy from anywhere or anyone. Take, for example, someone who is depressed, tired, and not feeling very well for whatever reason. She may walk into a room filled with sincerely happy people, and her mood becomes uplifted. Or you may have one friend who always gives you peace of mind. That's you absorbing positive vibrations.

However, emotions during a full Moon are very strong. People who put out negative vibrations tend to be more resilient than those who are joyous but more mild in nature. It's not that "happy people" are weaker; it's that they aren't focused on constantly putting up their armor of psychic protection when "negative people" are emanating negativity so intensely that it expands.

Moon Sensitive People

Have you ever walked into a room, and although the people inside—let's say a couple—appeared to be happy and getting along, you just felt there was something wrong because you could sense underlying tension? Or have you ever felt happy, but then a conversation with someone on the phone or via text made you feel depleted? These people are energy vampires, and they don't even know it. Are you someone who picks up negative energy like this regularly? If so, you might be full Moon sensitive. If you can shrug off negativity, you might be full Moon tolerant. Not sure where you fall on the spectrum? Break out that journal and observe your moods around the time of the full Moon.

If you are "full Moon sensitive," you can absorb its energy like a sponge. Even on a night when there is no visible full Moon, you can still be affected by its energy. The full Moon has the ability to open us up even more to the saturation of negative sensations.

Someone who is Moon sensitive typically becomes overemotional, depressed, discouraged, tired, easily temperamental, and has a lot of up-and-down shifts in energy at the time of a full Moon. You may become a drama queen or king during this phase. You break up with a significant other because he or she did something minor, or you may have a meltdown when the food you ordered in a restaurant isn't completely perfect.

Pay attention to your mood and disposition around a full Moon. Note mood swings and general changes in attitude that you just can't pinpoint to a direct cause. Do you have a pattern around this phase that makes you act differently? If so, you may be Moon sensitive.

Some people who are Moon sensitive have learned to manage it by simply visualizing a white light of protection around themselves as a psychic shield. You can try this at home: just envision a white bubble, balloon, or aura of white light around you. This visualization is a simple form of protection against darts of negativity from others (those energy vampires) coming at you. This technique will help you manage some of the more difficult situations you might encounter, but it does not turn you suddenly into a full Moon tolerant.

Moon Tolerant People

Some people can harness the energy of the full Moon and just get on with their lives. They are "Moon tolerant" people. Does that make them spiritually or psychically more advanced? Not at all. It just means that things roll off their backs more easily, including lunar energy.

Someone who is Moon tolerant is typically low-key, logical almost to a fault, has no energy spikes, and can whisk away negative events with words like, "I am not getting upset about this because everything happens for a higher purpose."

• • •

However you decide to practice your Moon magic—by meditation, celebration, or planting in the moonlight—be prepared to engage your energy and let the Moon take it where it will!

CHAPTER 6

HEALING BY THE PHASES OF THE MOON

This information is meant to be a discussion of celestial nature and its effects on health and is not meant to replace medical advice or your relationship with your physician. I share this with you because others have found this information helpful in their lives over many, many years, but a consultation with a qualified healthcare professional is always the safest bet if your ailments aren't going away or are getting worse. Better safe than sorry!

And please, please, please bear in mind, that when it comes to a medical emergency, do what needs to be done ASAP. Visualize yourself surrounded by a blue light, which is a healing light, and visualize yourself healthy.

Using Moon Phases to Plan Medical Procedures

The Moon has such a profound influence that it is extremely important to work *with* it—not against it—when it comes to our physical conditions. That's why the phases of the Moon are something to consider when you are looking into surgeries, medical procedures, and even emotional needs.

Our ancestors often used almanacs to determine the best time to undergo procedures or treatments—not only according to the waxing and the waning of the Moon but also according to which zodiac sign the Moon was in. Some people think of this technique as a superstition, but often the biggest doubters come to believe in these methods once they give them a chance. These skeptics-turned-believers base their trust on their own experiences and encounters, or on conversations with others who can vouch for the advantages of celestial influences.

Before getting into the astrological side of the Moon, let's talk about the general Moon stages and how they relate to the timing of medical procedures.

Full Moon

Full Moons are not considered a good time to have surgeries or medical procedures, as some people claim that blood reacts to the gravitational pull of the Moon. (Plasma, the liquid portion of blood, is 92 percent water.) You might also want to avoid three to five days *before* a full Moon and three to five days *after* a full Moon, as procedures on these days could lead to more blood loss and swelling.

Waning Moon

The waning Moon (when it looks like it is diminishing in the sky between its new and full phases) is considered the best phase of the Moon for an elective surgery, which is a procedure you can book in advance and is not an emergency. (Keep in mind, however, to avoid those three to five days before and after the full Moon, as was just mentioned.) If you are getting rid of anything in the body, do it under a waning Moon.

Waxing Moon

When the Moon waxes (appears as though it is expanding), it is a good time to get stronger. It is an agreeable time to add to your body. If you are "removing and replacing" (like a joint replacement or a heart valve), do it during a waxing Moon. The same goes for getting breast or dental implants (but again, not too close to a full Moon).

Mercury Retrograde

Have you every heard anyone say, "Mercury is retrograde; no wonder nothing is going right"? Mercury is moving in a retrograde manner—a motion that makes it appear to be going backward in the night sky. This happens three times a year for approximately three weeks at a time. The planet Mercury rules communication, travel, contracts, and so on. When Mercury is retrograde, communications systems go awry, machines break down, cell phones get lost, you text the wrong person, and boy oh boy, are you in trouble.

Well, this retrograde lunacy should be taken into consideration when timing your health procedures. When "Mercury goes retrograde," as some say, you should try to avoid this time frame when booking your surgery dates, procedural dates, doctors' visits, and even routine bloodwork. Take note that Mercury not only rules communication, but it also influences recall, technology, brainpower, and transportation. (Airport delays that were unexpected during perfect weather, blood specimens that were sent to the wrong lab, test results that were never sent to your doctor… Hmmm…was Mercury retrograde?)

Is there any good in Mercury retrograde? Of course. When it comes to emotional healing, Mercury retrograde can be good. It is thought by many astrologers that this is a beneficial time to revisit an old issue or connect to someone from the past who you had issues with so you can make peace and move on—even if it is just in your own mind or meditations. It is thought that after you revisit a situation during this time, you will be able to release it more readily. Mercury retrograde is not a time to reunite with someone for a relationship of any kind; rather, it's a time for achieving closure to something that may have been disturbing you on and off for a while.

Sign of the Right Time

Being aware of how the phases of the Moon can affect your health is a great start, but the Moon phases must ultimately be synced up with the appropriate zodiac signs to get maximum benefit. Your health is everything, after all, and anything that helps you prepare and plan for feeling your best is important to take into consideration.

I was always a believer in astrology but was never really totally engrossed by it. Then after doing some research many Moons ago, I recognized it can make a difference in many areas, including health. I hadn't given astrology all the credit it was due! Astrology is a tool for many situations, and for our purposes here, we'll use it to determine the best times for operations, medical appointments, bloodwork, and just about anything relating to a healthier and better body.

Let's start with the basics: each sign of the Western astrological zodiac rules specific parts of the body, including our organs. They are as follows:

- **ARIES** corresponds to the head, the eyes, and the nose. This is essentially the face.
- **TAURUS** corresponds to the throat, mouth, thyroid, tonsils, back of the head, ears, teeth, and jaw. The larynx and cerebellum, the part of the brain at the back of the skull, are also included.
- **GEMINI** rules the arms, shoulders, hands, lungs, thymus, upper ribs, and nervous system.
- **CANCER** influences the stomach, diaphragm, thorax, abdomen, breast, upper liver lobes, mammary glands, lower lung lobes, and the aorta, which is the main artery of the body.
- **LEO** corresponds to the heart, back, spine, arteries, and circulation.
- **VIRGO** holds sway over the digestive system, gall bladder, intestines, spleen, lower liver lobes, pancreas, and nervous system.
- **LIBRA** influences the skin, buttocks, loins, inguinal region (groin), kidneys, and vascular nerve system.
- **SCORPIO** rules the reproductive system, sexual organs, bowels, bladder, urethra, prostate, rectum, descending colon, and excretory system, which is generally responsible for releasing bodily wastes.

- **SAGITTARIUS** oversees the upper half of the lower extremities (hips and thighs), liver, arteries, veins, and sciatic nerve.
- **CAPRICORN** rules the knees, skin, joints, and skeletal system. Some include the teeth in the sign of Capricorn.
- **AQUARIUS** influences the circulatory system, lower legs, lower half of lower extremities, and ankles.
- **PISCES** corresponds to the feet, toes, circulatory system, and immune system.

Here is where this knowledge will come into play as far as planning, scheduling, and developing good health for an optimal life.

The magic is that every 2.5 days, the Moon moves through one of the twelve signs of the zodiac (or constellations). To find out which sign the Moon is in on any given day, consult http://lunarliving.org/moonsigns.html. You'll find lots of information on their Moon signs page.

In my opinion, the most important rule is that you NEVER have surgery or a procedure when the Moon is in the sign that corresponds to the part of body that is going to be operated on or manipulated. There is a strain put on that body part when the Moon is in that sign; hence, it's not a good time to irritate it. There is a quote attributed to Hippocrates, an ancient Greek physician regarded as the father of medicine: "Do not touch with iron those parts of the body that are governed by the sign through which the Moon is passing." In this day and age, we can translate the "iron" to mean a scalpel and assume he is telling us not to have surgery on the day that the Moon is in ("passing through") the sign that corresponds to that body part. For example: Pisces corresponds to the feet and toes. You do not want to have your bunions removed when the Moon is in Pisces!

Take into account when going through the following list that these are broad views and not detailed breakdowns. If you have an unusual illness that you are dealing with, consult a professional astrologer for assistance working with your chart for a precise conclusion.

- **MOON IN ARIES:** Avoid tooth extractions or invasive oral surgery including the jaw. Do not operate on the eyes, head, or brain.
- **MOON IN TAURUS:** Avoid surgery on the cerebellum, which is the part of the brain that is responsible for motor movement and coordination. Stay clear of neck and throat surgery, which includes tonsils, vocal cords, and the thyroid gland.
- **MOON IN GEMINI:** Avoid surgery of the lungs and amputations of the arms or hands at this time.
- **MOON IN CANCER:** Avoid having surgery that opens the thorax or rib cage. Stay away from surgeries for diseases that involve the digestive organs.
- **MOON IN LEO:** Avoid surgery on the heart, back muscles, and spinal cord.
- **MOON VIRGO:** Avoid surgery on the abdomen.
- **MOON IN LIBRA:** Avoid kidney surgery.
- **MOON IN SCORPIO:** Avoid hemorrhoid surgery, hernia and appendix surgery, and generally avoid cutting in the groin area. Stay away from procedures involving the urinary and sexual organs.
- **MOON IN SAGITTARIUS:** Avoid a hip replacement or leg amputation, as well as surgery on a femoral hernia.
- **MOON IN CAPRICORN:** Avoid knee and shin surgery, in addition to skin procedures.
- **MOON IN AQUARIUS:** Avoid surgeries on varicose veins, the calves, and the eyes.
- **MOON IN PISCES:** Avoid surgery of the feet, toes, abdomen, and lungs.

Void of Course

There are other complicated things to think about as well when you are using the Moon as a guide—when the Moon is "void of course" (VOC), for example. This term basically refers to when the Moon is transitioning from one astrological sign to another. This period might take only a few minutes, a few hours, or sometimes a whole day. Some feel that during this time, the Moon is in no sign at all, meaning nothing you want will happen—it's in a void.

The basic rule regarding health and surgical treatments is that when you want something to happen successfully, avoid the VOC Moon periods or there is huge potential a procedure may have to be done all over again. To find when the Moon is void of course, consult astrology calendars or almanacs and do some Internet searches using an exact date.

Birth

Not every medical issue is a major worry. There are some fun aspects of health that we look forward to as well, such as having babies. What if you want to have a baby boy after having three girls? Can the Moon help you with that? Some say it's Moon lore, and some say it's scientifically proven, but whatever the case, it's fun to try!

It is whispered in secret (why, I don't know; I guess because sex is involved) that if you conceive a child when the Moon is traveling through a particular sign of the zodiac, you can predict if it will be a boy or girl. The masculine signs of the zodiac are Aries, Gemini, Leo, Libra, Sagittarius, and Aquarius. The feminine signs are Taurus, Cancer, Virgo, Scorpio, Capricorn and Pisces.

If the child is conceived when the Moon is in a masculine sign, you will have a boy. If it is conceived when the Moon is in a feminine sign, it will be a girl. (Don't ask me about twins. Maybe if the signs are ready to change, you can have one of each. That's just a guess.) If you already have children and remember when they were conceived, go back and find out what sign the Moon was in at the time to test the theory!

• • •

So much healing and so little time! You can see how this can become complicated—the phases of the Moon and the zodiac signs....Is the Moon void of course or is Mercury retrograde? Holy Moon madness! Let's put my earlier recommendations in a lunar nutshell:

- Generally, don't have surgery of any kind five days before or five days after a full Moon.
- If something has to be removed, do it under a waning Moon.
- If something has to be removed and replaced, do it under a waxing Moon.
- If something has to be added, also look to the waxing Moon phase.
- Don't have surgeries or medical procedures when the Moon is void of course or when Mercury is retrograde.

CHAPTER 7

LEARNING TO MEDITATE

The Many Benefits of Meditation

Meditation encompasses a wide variety of consciousness practices designed to still the mind and access a deeper part of the human consciousness. Now considered an essential part of well-being, it requires the ability to free one's attention from life's distractions and quiet down chaotic and restless thinking. It's possible to soak up lunar energy through meditation during any phase of the Moon.

Meditation, when done correctly, allows you to cultivate mindfulness and healthfully achieve an altered state of consciousness. An altered state of consciousness, meanwhile, provides fresh perspectives and new insights for solving problems and advancing self-awareness and inner growth. It also can be a way to cast your intentions to the universal life force in order to bring forth better days.

The benefits of meditation are found in abundance in newspaper articles, television segments, blogs, and through word of mouth. With regular practice, the body, mind, and soul are transformed by meditation. Some benefits are experienced almost immediately while others unfold progressively and may take more time to become apparent. Connecting with the innermost aspect of your being offers a wealth of benefits:

- Promotes relaxation
- Aids mind and body healing
- Renews mental and physical energy
- Enables problem-solving and resilience
- Engenders compassion, patience, generosity, love, and forgiveness

For anyone who is hesitant to really dive into meditation or has never even tried it, keep an open mind. If you don't try, how will you know?

Maybe you have attempted meditating and think that it just doesn't work for you. I remember a time when I would lie on my bed and attempt to meditate but instead fall asleep. Then I moved to the floor in my living room and still fell asleep. Finally, I went outside, sat on the grass, and it was a totally different experience indeed. This time I fell asleep and had bug bites to boot! After the itching stopped, I started to think about those who came before me and their meditation practices (or whatever they may have called it). They had bugs, they needed sleep…so what did they do? Well, I'm not sure I ever came up with an answer, but it did cause me to dive a little deeper into different methods of meditation—so I could stay awake!

The Origins of Meditation

Ancient meditation practices are found in virtually all cultures across the globe, predating all world religions. Although methods vary from culture to culture, meditation is considered an essential aspect of spiritual development.

"When you are with someone you love very much, you can talk and it is pleasant, but the reality is not in the conversation. It is simply in being together. Meditation is the highest form of prayer. In it you are so close to God that you don't need to say a thing. It's just great to be together."

—SWAMI CHETANANANDA

Most religions feature a form of meditation that embraces communing with the Oneness of All Creation, Brahman, God, Allah, the Great Mystery, the Infinite Creator, a higher power, Source, the Great Spirit, or whatever term you prefer to describe that which is beyond naming. In my observations, prayer and meditation are similar in that they involve spending time in silent reflection communing with a higher being.

Early Meditators

Even prehistoric people knew what Albert Einstein would later elucidate, "No problem can be solved from the same level of consciousness that created it." According to some archaeologists and anthropologists, there is reason to believe shamans engaged in practices 30,000 years ago that were the precursors to modern systems of meditation and yoga. Since then, shamans across the globe have used rhythmic drumming, chanting, dancing, and psychoactive plants to enter altered states of consciousness. They did this to heal, obtain knowledge, and restore wholeness and balance by reuniting the soul with the Infinite Spirit.

Markings on antlers and bones found at cave ritual sites indicate that early humans tracked the phases of the Moon and suggest that many shamanic and ceremonial activities had a seasonal or periodic orientation related to the lunar cycle. Stonehenge, built in prehistoric England, and similar sites around the globe were set up for the purpose of measuring cosmic movement and marking equinoxes, solstices, and lunar eclipses.

Preparing for Your Meditation Practice

A thoughtful Moon meditation practice can be amazing and transforming when you're motivated to do it. Living in a universe where everything is in constant motion, and in a period of history when technology is accelerating every facet of our lives, it's very challenging (but rewarding!) to achieve stillness for even a few seconds. (My beloved readers, that means no texting by the light of the silvery Moon! Leave electronics out of your meditation entirely.)

So let's do a little Moon meditation preparation. First of all, remember to keep preparations simple, relaxing, and enjoyable. Any activity that helps clear away the chatter in your mind and ease bodily tensions will go a long way in helping you experience a deep, restorative, and blissful meditation. (For those of you who already are good meditators, you can appreciate what is was like when you first began. Just review the information in this chapter and move forward to the meditations part of the book.) Here are some guidelines for readying yourself for lunar meditation.

Eat Well Ahead of Time

Unless your hunger will be distracting, it's probably best to avoid eating for an hour before meditating. If you must eat, make it a light snack, like fruit, so your energy is available to elevate your consciousness rather than digest food. If you eat heavy food or a large meal, you could end up feeling sleepy and find it difficult to sit comfortably or maintain your focus for any length of time. (I think that is what used to happen to me.)

Take a Shower or Bath

If time allows, you may want to include showering or bathing as part of your preparation routine. The act of washing has long been a symbol of cleansing and purification. It can be refreshing and have a positive effect on your mood and mind-set. A stimulating shower will saturate your body with calming negative ions, and a bath will soak away muscular tension, leaving you soothed and mentally relaxed.

Dress Comfortably

Although high-end yoga and meditation clothes are now considered trendy, meditation only requires that you dress for maximum comfort. For most people, this means lightweight, loose-fitting clothes. If you are inside, a big old T-shirt and your underwear will do just fine. (But do wear clothing outside. It just is better all the way around!)

Practice Yoga to De-Stress

Shake off stress. Stress is not a purely psychological phenomenon. It runs through your entire nervous system. It constricts circulation, binds muscles, and impacts the functioning of organs throughout your body. Any physical activity that relieves stress and encourages circulation will help you meditate more deeply. Yoga is especially perfect for relieving stress. This is what makes yoga and meditation the perfect combination and explains why yoga is called "moving meditation."

If you are not a "yoga person," just give a shake of the hands and think about shaking off negativity. Visualize it. See a gray color coming out of your hands and going up and away from you. Remember, everything is intention.

Find a Suitable Space

Set the mood and create a relaxing atmosphere in a place where you won't be distracted. Think of it as sacred space where you will entertain the Divine Spirit. Choose an open space with plenty of air and energy circulation, if such a place is available. If you are outside, be in a place that is safe and feels comfortable. If you live in a small apartment and the air isn't that great or maybe there aren't many windows…no worries. Put a pretty picture in front of you to focus your attention on—how about a Moon picture? (No money to buy a picture? Draw one yourself. There is always a way. Who knows, you might discover you are an artist!) And please put pets in a different space unless they help you meditate.

Consider pleasing your senses of hearing and smell by bumping up the atmosphere with aromatherapy and meditation music or sounds of nature that relax you. If you are already outside in nature, you don't need these things. Dab on or spritz the space with your favorite scent, light a fragrant candle, or burn a little incense to create the perfect sanctuary for peaceful meditation.

Above all: know yourself. Incense makes me sneeze, so obviously I don't use it as part of my practice! Don't do something just because it works for other people. Try it and if it's not for you, that's okay.

Choose a Comfortable Meditation Posture

Select a posture that works best for you. Meditation can be done in one of four postures: standing, sitting, lying, or walking.

- **LYING:** Meditation masters agree that lying down to meditate is not optimal. This is because our energy diffuses and creates deep overall bodily relaxation that often leads to sleep rather than meditative mindfulness. Therefore, a recumbent position is best used in preparation for or waking from sleep. However, for those of us who can fight the urge to doze, it is a good position for calming and revitalizing our senses as well as rebalancing and restoring energetic flow to the nervous system. To accomplish this, lie flat on a wide and tall surface with your arms outstretched and the palms of each hand facing upward. Alternatively, raise your knees to form low mountain peaks while keeping your feet evenly spaced, about a hip-width apart, and flat on the floor. Or place your legs at a 90-degree angle onto a chair or couch. Remember to keep your spine straight. Close your eyes. Stretch, scan the body, and release any tension. Breathe deeply, slowly, and consistently. Open to, immerse in, and receive restorative, healing energy.
- **WALKING:** You can pace or walk in a circle if it helps you focus and you don't get dizzy. Experiment a little if you're not sure.
- **SITTING:** Generally, sitting is the optimal position. You can sit on the floor or in a chair, whichever is most comfortable. Sitting provides the perfect balance of focus and relaxation, or at least the potential for it, because when the body is upright, both the body and mind tend to be alert and attentive.

- **STANDING:** As for standing, most people feel too tense and bored standing in one place for more than a few minutes, but if it works for you, go for it!

Remember the Moon Phases

Always, keep your simple lunar systems in mind:

- Trying to release anything or anyone? Use a waning Moon.
- Want to put something in your life, like a new home, career, mate, or even pet? Look to a waxing Moon.
- Want to discard something in your life, like an illness, etc.? Think dark Moon, when there is no visible Moon for us to see on Earth.
- The full Moon is best for anything of an intuitive nature, like fortune-telling or spellcasting (for those who do it—in a positive way, of course). In addition, it's a good time to renew commitments to projects or people.

A Simple Breathing Exercise to Do Before Meditation

Once you are in your special space and are in position, center yourself by taking a moment to slow down the pace. Do some slow, deep breathing before you begin to meditate. Many use their breath as a focal point and follow each inhalation and exhalation with their mind. Follow these steps:

1. Tune into your breath. Simply focus your attention on it.
2. Take an exaggerated breath: a deep inhale through your nostrils (three seconds), hold your breath (two seconds), and a long exhale through your mouth (four seconds).
3. Then observe the pattern of your breath, the inhale and exhale, with your mind. Feel the natural flow of your breath. Notice where you feel your breath in your body and when one breath ends and the next

begins. No need to adjust it. Just observe. It may help to focus on the rise and fall of your chest or the sensation through your nostrils.

4. Concentrate on breathing in and out. You will immediately feel yourself start to relax.

After this exercise, you will be ready to focus on the meditations for what you want, which are addressed in Part 3.

Another Pre-Meditation Calming Technique

Focusing on breath and breathing is excellent, but it doesn't always work for everyone. (Yes, I know. I always take the easy way, but I don't think I was put on this planet to do things that I am not comfortable with, and you shouldn't feel obligated either.) In other areas of life, it can be good to be pulled out of your comfort zone, think outside the box, and so forth. But when it comes to meditation, this philosophy only adds more stress, which is just what you are trying to get rid of.

Therefore, I have a technique that works for me and others that you might want to experiment with. Keep in mind this kind of meditation is about focusing on the phases of the Moon in which you want to achieve something.

1. Sit in a chair or lie down and see a white light at your feet. If you are doing something that involves healing, I suggest visualizing a blue light, as that is the color of healing.
2. See the white light slowly covering your toes, your ankles, your calves, knees, and so forth till you get to the top of your head. When you get to your arms, include them in your torso so that the white light surrounds your body widthwise as well.

If this method works for you, it should put you in an altered state of consciousness.

As noted previously, this is where your affirmations or statements will take place.

Steps to Ending a Meditation

Once you have completed your Moon meditation, you need to slowly refocus or come down. Since it takes a few moments to return and re-sync consciousness with the body, you'll always want to give yourself some time to exit a Moon meditation session.

Follow these steps:

1. Become aware and notice that you are ready to end the meditation. With this intention, the body will shift into a neutral state of readiness.
2. Give your consciousness a minute or two to coast and then settle back into the body.
3. Once settled in, start making small movements and sounds. You may want to sigh. Wait a few seconds between movements and sighs. You will feel your energy increase and your metabolism begin to reignite.
4. Open your eyes a little, then close them again; be present for and notice your inner feelings.

This end-of-session interlude is your transition back into your body and return to an active state. (The primary objective of meditation is to carry the relaxed awareness and attentiveness into action.)

• • •

The ideas in this chapter should give you a suitable design for how exactly you will be meditating.

CHAPTER 8

THE POWER OF INTENTION SETTING

Connecting the Moon to Your Intentions

An intention is a goal, purpose, or plan that you focus on with great concentration. One single thing done with intention is better than doing many things without it. I know many people who set their goals via intentions, the law of attraction, meditation, or any number of methods alone. I suggest that you can use any—or all—of these methods in unison to achieve a truly powerful visualization of what you want.

When you use the Moon to set an intention, you are aiming for a target or goal, which is something people do every day. The difference is that you are using the phases of the Moon as a timing tool to achieve that goal. In fact, it's a huge advantage.

How to Set an Intention

The following are a few steps you can employ to set an intention.

Write It Down

I advise writing down intentions to sort them out and truly set them in your mind. I will say this several times in this book: keep the high-tech devices out of it. Smartphones and the like can have a great place in your life, but sometimes it's better to simplify things and just use a piece of paper and a pencil or pen. Bonus points for using a decent piece of paper and not a cocktail napkin.

Most people agree that writing things down acts as an appeal to the subconscious mind. The problem is, they don't seem to follow through on their end of things. It's like dieting. People know they should eat this or that because it's healthy, but they fail when it comes to putting healthy habits into action and ultimately continue to maintain unhealthy behaviors. You know better, but you do it anyway. The good news is that once you are aware of it—which you can indicate by writing it down—you will do it less and less.

Writing something down takes it off your mind and gives you a moment to breathe and not worry so much about what you want to happen. It takes your desire into the physical and out of the emotional and mental. Your intentions allow you to set the course of your life by putting out into the universe what you want to see happen. Worry, by itself, is unproductive and can actually perpetuate your situation. If you are forever thinking, "I have no money, I never pay my rent on time, I will never be able to pay off that loan," and so forth, you are programming the universe to give you exactly what you are thinking about. You will stay in that mode. Thoughts turn into things. So think about your intentions instead of your problems.

If you frequently moan, "I don't have a mate in my life." The universe says, "Okay, if that's what you want, I will make it so." By focusing on your problems instead of your solutions, you are attracting all those things you don't want.

Be Realistic

Remember, when you set an intention, you need to truly want it, and you need to know it's realistic. I can wish to turn into a fish so I can just swim around all day, but we all know that's just not ever going to happen. So, first things first: intentions must be based in reality.

Be Ready

You also have to be in a place in your life where you are ready to receive what you're asking for. If you are twenty-five years old and asking for a spouse, four kids, and a house...but you know that you also want to travel the world and have a high-profile career...those are conflicting ideas. You can do it all—you just can't do it all at once, so choose what you want *now*.

Stay Focused

Keep track of what you're asking for and notice whether any newer intentions conflict with other intentions you may have already set. There is no universal law that says you can't back off an intention that no longer suits you, but you should be aware that it's not a good idea to request things that can't possibly work together (like "I really want a job in the city," and "I really want to work on a goat farm").

Decide on one or two intentions at a time. Don't write down dozens of things, like, "I want a better job, a new love, a new house, and to lose weight. Oh wait, and I could use a new car—and those shoes at the shoe store to go on sale. Better yet, just have those new heels arrive at my front door. Anything else? Oh yeah, I also want to be invited to that party on Saturday. One last thing, Moon, I would also like my skin to clear up and those anxiety attacks to go away."

Stop the Moon madness! That's just too much. One thing at a time. You might be able to throw in two desires if they are related, such as finding a new job and getting a raise. If it feels like too many requests are coming forth from your brain at the same time, then trim them down! You will know when you are not being reasonable. You will feel it. Get specific with fewer requests—something like, "I see myself in a new job in the advertising field, at ABC Advertising on Main Street in an executive position. No more working on Saturdays and no more promised promotions that don't seem to come to fruition." That's a lot of particulars, but it is all about one thing: finding a new career.

WORKSHEET: SET AN INTENTION

Here is a worksheet that you can do to make the intention-setting process stress-free. You can make a copy of this form or just rewrite it using lined paper. Leave lots of lines or space for your writing.

1. Write down your intention.

   ____

   ____

2. Select the right Moon phase that suits your intention, be it full, waning, dark, new, or waxing.

   ____

   ____

3. Select your Moon meditation (see Chapters 11–14) or create your own.

   ____

   ____

4. Review your written information every day and make notes of anything that is happening that relates to your intention coming to fruition.

This worksheet will help keep you on track as you wait for the universe to manifest your intentions!

Be Specific

Here's an example of a less-than-ideal intention: "I want to find a loving partner." Why is it "wrong"? It's too short and lacks details.

Instead, be more specific: "I want to find a loving partner in the next two months who lives within two hours of me, is like-minded, likes dogs, and is good-natured and financially secure or has potential of becoming such."

You can put physical aspects in here if you like, such as age, hair color (or no hair at all), and so forth. It may seem like a lot of detail, but it stays within the category of finding a mate.

• • •

It's amazing when you set your intentions the release in has on you. There is a peacefulness in knowing that you have done something to achieve your purpose.

CHAPTER 9

MANIFESTING YOUR INTENTIONS

The Importance of Passion

To bring your intentions or dreams to fruition, you must first have a solid intention, which we discussed in Chapter 8. But there is a difference between having an intention and *manifesting* one. Often, the difference comes down to passion.

Let's say you have every intention of doing the laundry before Friday. That may be your intention, but if you're not passionate about it, you might procrastinate and not do it. Or maybe you will shave that intention down a bit and only wash the clothes you *really* need and figure you will do the rest some other time.

Most of us can agree that doing the laundry is not anything to get excited over. Many of us have loftier goals, like becoming a singer or the CEO of a successful business, and we get enthusiastic about those ideas. So those are the things I want you to focus on when you're thinking about manifesting intentions. There are no limits here! Imagine you can have anything you want: any job, a relationship, a new house, etc. You can use the power of the Moon's phases to help bring those things into your life.

It is important to be very clear about what you want and the outcome you expect. Motivation is important. Doing laundry doesn't motivate me, for example, but having a new kitchen does, and selling books can help me to do that. I wanted to write a book, so I set my intention, used the Moon phases to help bring it about, and *voila*! Here we are!

How to Manifest Your Intention, Step by Step

There are three rules for manifesting anything:

1. Ask
2. Believe (as in believe it will be yours)
3. Receive

You can't do just one or two of the three. You must know in your heart that all three are truth. To manifest an intention, there are some rather simple steps to follow alongside these rules. Let's go into each step in greater detail.

Step 1: Identify What You Want (Ask)

What is it you really want? If you are really stuck on this question, go back to Chapter 8 and use the information there to flesh out your desires. Keep in mind that it does not have to be your ultimate life goal; it can be something that you feel you want in your life now, like a new car or a new pair of shoes. Sometimes it's best to start manifesting smaller, tangible things so that you can build your confidence in your practice.

Example: I want to find a job that allows me to travel more.

Okay, wonderful. You have identified a goal.

Now we'll take things a step farther. Ask yourself *why* you want it. Be very honest with your answer: why do you want to travel?

Your answer might be, "I want to travel because I am looking for love, and I never meet anyone here. Maybe if I am exposed to more people in different settings, I will meet someone interesting and can move out of this city I hate."

Or, "I want to travel because I want to get out of the house. My partner drives me crazy, and I really don't know if I should stay in this relationship."

There are many reasons behind your intentions that you may not be admitting to yourself. You must identify why you are asking for a particular outcome. "It will make me happy" is not the answer. *Why* will it make you happy? It is very important that you are clear and sure about what you want to achieve or you could end up accidentally pointing yourself in the wrong direction.

Step 2: Do It Your Way (Ask/Believe)

Once you set your intention and determine why you want it, you have to come up with a plan of action that works for you. Let's say your intention is to become a public speaker because your sister is making a fortune talking to groups about pet care. You think, "Well, it worked for her." Yes, it did, but that was *her* passion. Is it yours too? Maybe, maybe not.

Why can't you just copy other people's intentions? Because of that enthusiasm and passion I was talking about before. You can fake writing down an intention, but when it comes to manifesting, the universe knows whether you're sincere. You can't just go through the motions. In this example, if you were just going to follow in your sister's footsteps without any excitement for the job except for the paycheck, your career would end up very different from hers. And if you were truly passionate about lecturing about animals, you still wouldn't have to do everything exactly the way she did to be successful.

Start to Get Focused on Specifics

You should design a unique plan of action just for you. You can also combine methods. Modify a proven concept of achieving your intention.

For example, some people will find that simply getting into a meditative state works well for manifesting an intention. Others find that in order to achieve that meditative state, they need to burn incense or take a walk in nature or create a vision board to focus on during their meditation. What's important is setting an intention that's right for you: maybe your sister went to school for a master's degree in public communication, but you are a naturally gifted speaker and you only need to find some smaller speaking gigs to get you started. Think about what skills or finances you will need to make this work. How will you acquire those skills or finances, or do you already have them?

Let's begin to think about the Moon. You'll need a lunar calendar that includes not only the present month but also the months ahead for the coming year. If you print out one month at a time from an online calendar, you're thinking too much in the present. (And yes, I believe in living in the now, but at the moment we're planning to use the cycles of the Moon.)

Make a list of things you want to achieve within the next month and year. These are a little different from intentions, simply because you're not putting all of your energy into making a list—this is more of a wish list of things you may want to focus your energy on. And as we all know, our energy can only go in so many directions at one time. Be realistic. If you want to lose forty pounds, we all know that can't happen from one full Moon to the next. If you want to go to college and get a degree, that is not going to happen in two or three months. You know what is realistic and not. This is not the same concept as a genie in a lamp; this is working with nature.

Next, plan to make a plan. Do it on a day or night when you have time and no distractions. (A waxing Moon or a full Moon is great.) Sit at a table, on the sofa, or somewhere that feels relaxing to you.

Work Alone

Though it might be tempting to involve a friend in this process, it's not usually a good idea to do so. Asking a friend questions like, "What should I plan for?" "What do you think I should do?" when you're working on a personal goal is not conducive to a productive outcome. This has to come from you. If you want to show it to someone afterward, you can, but at the outset, write it by yourself. Have faith in yourself. No one knows you better than you do. Sure, they might know your past or what you "say" you want or need. But you alone know your heart.

Sometimes friends can be helpful at pointing out the obvious, like how you always *say* you're going to get organized and then you forget about it. But if you want to become a chef at a restaurant and your friend reminds you that you have a college degree in teaching and insists you must be crazy for thinking you can change career paths now, that can be a negative influence on your planning. Don't let someone steal your dreams. Be ready to get past those types of doubts: maybe you can teach and cook while you transition from one career to the other. That's where your plan comes in: "I will teach for another year while I am taking culinary classes and then find a part-time job at a restaurant." You will feel so good just making the plan at first. It gives you direction, and you have started the process. To some it may not be much, but it is more than you think. You have lifted the burden of not knowing what is going to happen in the future. You have a plan.

The only time you might want to set goals with a friend sitting next to you is if you are planning something the two of you will do together, like taking a trip or going to a yoga class. Even then, the ideal method would be to call your friend in advance and ask which days are good for her to participate in the planning process. Ask for at least five days so you can check the skies. Beyond that, you should work alone, using your own insight.

Step 3: Work with the Moon (Ask)

Okay, you've also followed the advice in Chapter 8 about setting your intentions. You have decided what your intention or dream is going to be, you've checked in with yourself and your motivations, and you feel that, yes, this is a good idea and you want it for the right reasons. You've determined how you can make this plan happen. Now you know what you're asking for, it's time to shoot for the Moon.

Always make sure you're working within the correct Moon phase:

- If you are looking to add or expand something in your life, you want to ask for it during a waxing Moon.
- If you want to eliminate something, do it during a waning Moon.
- If you want to work on a long-term goal, plan for a blue Moon, which gives you a much wider window of energy.
- Take action on a new Moon (crescent Moon or waxing Moon).

Sample Timeline

Note: the following dates are just examples to give you an idea of how your plan might look.

NOV 23: DARK MOON: (no visible light in the sky): I will decide when to make my plan when the Moon is dark because it will be a good time for contemplation.

NOV 26: NEW MOON: I will write down my plan.

DEC 2: WAXING MOON: I will take action on doing at least one thing that will take me another step toward my target.

DEC 4: WAXING MOON: I will take another specific action toward helping me reach my aspiration.

DEC 8: FULL MOON: I will reflect on what I have accomplished so far and celebrate. If I haven't achieved anything as of yet, I will do something different so I can achieve my goal when the Moon is waxing again. (Write it down.)

DEC 13: WANING MOON: I will release the thing that has been stopping me from my goal.

DEC 21: DARK MOON: I will rest and decide what my next plan of action is going to be by looking at what I wrote on November 26 and during the full Moon.

Naturally, you can tweak this and work with the days you have available. The important thing is to stick to your phases:

- **NEW MOON:** Plan.
- **WANING MOON:** Release things that are stopping you.
- **DARK MOON:** Reflect, celebrate, and/or plan even more.
- **NEW MOON OR WAXING MOON:** Take action and move forward.

Step 4: Meditate on It (Believe)

Practice the Moon meditations that guide you with the right words, atmosphere, and thought process to put forth your intention to that higher power. Close your session with powerful words, such as, "Let it be" or "And so it is." This means you are not messing around! You are expecting results!

Following Your Moods

Although all of this planning and scheduling sounds good in theory, there can be a few bumps on the path to the new or better you. You can meditate on overcoming obstacles or setbacks under any phase of the Moon, but what happens when nature doesn't want to cooperate? Can the Moon be moody?

The Moon isn't really moody per se, but you can be. The Moon phases repeat themselves every 29.5 days, so there is no real guessing about which phase is which and which of those phases work well with each part of your plan.

There comes a point where it's not only about the Moon phases; it's about you, yourself, and your moods. If the Moon is waxing and you "should" be good, happy, and enchanted with life, you might not be. You could have a waxing Moon with a dark Moon state of mind. But that's okay. Don't let the Moon oblige you to do something you planned on a certain day, month, or even hour if you are not in the right disposition to do so. Take your feelings on that given day and set the tone. Tired, crabby, or exhausted? Don't push yourself. It's all about you and achieving balance in life. To put more pressure on yourself because a full or new Moon only comes once a month defies common sense. You cannot predict when you'll be in a bad mood or have a headache, so you'll have to make adjustments to your plan to fit what your feelings are at the time.

Be flexible. Things happen. For example, if you like to do your Moon planning and meditation outdoors, great—but you can't control the elements. So there you are, all prepared for your big night of incorporating the Moon into your big plan. You have everything you need, and suddenly you feel a drip, drip, drip. No! It can't be rain.

Don't get discouraged (and don't sit on the ground when there is lightning).

That's the time to relax, have a sense of humor, and acknowledge that the Moon did nothing wrong. All you can control is your own mood. Look to your calendar for another time and, if need be, a different place. Or if possible, just go inside. It may not work if it happens to be your spouse's poker night and you were glad to have a good reason to sit outside by the light of the Moon.

The point is, the Moon is steady, but the weather and our moods are not necessarily in sync with that. Take a deep breath, keep your sense of humor, and remember that everything happens for a higher purpose. Do whatever it takes to not get too out of sorts.

Step 5: Check in Daily (Believe)

Review your written intention every day till you get to the full Moon. This can be a simple check-in with yourself and the universe—just a reminder that you are asking for something specific and that you *know* it will be delivered. On the day of the full Moon, review your intention one last time and then take it easy. Leave things to the universe and wait. Don't think about how long you will have to wait; just know things will transpire in a timely fashion. The less you contemplate "when" it will happen, the more you push away the temptation of skepticism, which inhibits believing.

Step 6: Acknowledge Your Progress (Receive)

Always take pride in your smallest accomplishment when you are manifesting your intention.

Say you have a new online shop selling handmade items. You sell one in two weeks. Don't look at the negative, saying, "I should have sold thirty by now." Look at the positive: It's a start and one sale can lead to many more. In short, it's an achievement. Be happy about it.

But also take action and revisit your original intention. How many had you planned on selling per week? Did you write that number down specifically, or did you simply write, "I want to sell a lot"? The beauty of working with the Moon's phases is that they are always coming back around, and if you find that you left out an important part of your plan for success, you can use the energy of the next waning or full Moon to add to your original request.

• • •

Draw on the lunar energy that works with your goal, and the universe will take it from there!

CHAPTER 10
CREATING VISION BOARDS

What Is a Vision Board?

A vision board is a tool that can help manifest what you want in life. It is literally a board, poster, or even a wall on which you can display words, photos, magazine images, or whatever visuals you'd like to assist in shaping your future around the things you want to achieve or attract. Some people think of it as a collage of things (or even feelings) that we want.

Along with all the pretty pictures and inspiring words, you'll use visualization techniques and intention setting to achieve these goals by looking at your board daily until the things on it become your reality. But first you have to create it—and I mean *physically* create it—using pens, paper, cardboard, tape, pictures, and the like.

Wait, wait, don't give up because you might have to go to your junk drawer to find scissors and glue! Hear me out. This is where I often perceive hesitation. Many people have heard of vision boards and know they have something to do with pictures and trying to get what you want. They think it's probably a good thing, but they don't even try because it seems like a lot of work. If you are that person, think outside the box for a moment.

I know you are thinking that you just don't have time, or you're saying to yourself, "A craft project? Ugh! I'm not creative." But if your life isn't exactly the way you want it right now, what do you have to lose? *Give it a go*. You know that saying, if you keep doing what you're doing, you'll keep getting what you're getting? So let's be open-minded and try something different.

For those of you who have already made vision boards and love them, or are just open-minded to them, you have taken the first step. (If your vision boards haven't worked in the past, I have a few tips and suggestions that might help you with that later.)

I'll show you two different types of vision boards you can create. You can also use your own method if you like. Some people separate their vision boards by having one specifically just for their career and a few others for their personal life, family life, vacations, and so forth. That is up to you, but having too many may end up being confusing, so be aware of how many you have going at any given time.

Designing a Classic Vision Board

Making a classic vision board is simple, and the design can be as simple or as elaborate as you choose to make it. Follow these steps to craft yours.

Decide When to Make Your Board

First of all, decide *when* you want to create your board. It does not have to be at the beginning of the year, for example, though many people make one then. You can create one whenever you feel like it or once your old one has accomplished its goal.

One thing to keep in mind: I believe you should make your vision board on a waxing Moon. That's when we want things to grow and get bigger and bigger. Even if you want to lose weight, when it comes to a vision board, think of the weight loss as increasing more and more, not what you see on the scale. It's all about how you "see things." Full Moons work too since they make us more sensitive to the things around us.

Gather Your Materials

Next, start collecting materials. Don't feel like you need to spend a lot of money or go out of your way to find special equipment. It's your board and no one can tell you how it should look except you. Everything you put into this board has to make you feel good and reinforce your intentions.

Backing

You can use a piece of paper, cardboard, a bulletin board and push pins, or Styrofoam as your backing. You can also make a frame on a wall with painter's tape, let's say about 12" × 12"—or larger if you have numerous ideas! If you want to get fancier, go for it. Get some good cardboard to work on and have it professionally framed.

Pictures and Words

Next, you'll need pictures. But pictures of what? If you know what direction you want to go in, you are lucky, and I call this a "classic vision board." Go through magazines, newspapers, images on the computer—even cut up your dog's big bag of dog food if the photo on it matches the new dog you want. But be specific: if you want a particular breed of dog, for example, find a picture of the breed, not just any old canine.

Take a label off a spice jar if it calls to mind your intention, or use an appliqué you had laying around to place on your board. This is where your creative side will kick in. You will surprise yourself at how inventive you can be. Of course, you can always draw something freehand, but I think a picture of the exact thing you want is best. If you want a red car but could only find a picture of a yellow one…be prepared to drive a yellow automobile.

Speaking of specific, if you want to get a raise, do not put a picture of a big pile of money on the board. Rather, write "$25.00 an hour" or "$250.00 an hour." Or cut out numbers and letters that say the same.

Want a romantic relationship or a friendship? Be specific. Don't cut out a picture of a celebrity unless that is truly realistic. Your subconscious knows.

If you're looking for more general things, look for inspirational words like *faith*, *gratitude*, *family*, and so on.

Arrange Your Pictures on the Board

Now take your pictures, words, and so forth and arrange them how you want them to appear. Shift things around as needed to get the aesthetic look you want. You do not have to have the pictures and words in any particular order. It is not intended to be a road map with a beginning picture and final image of a goal. Leave a little to the universe. Then use tape, glue, or push pins to adhere everything to whatever it is you are using for a board.

Keep it neat and organized. You don't want to invite chaos into the picture. Don't overlap and cram too many things on your board. If you overwhelm your board, you will be overwhelmed.

I have a friend who overlapped the pictures on her vision board. She thought it was beautiful—she had pictures of career moves, cats, houses, travel, and so on. All those things are absolutely fine. But let me tell you the rest of the story: she wanted a new home—it would be her first. She also wanted to have cats, which her present apartment in New York would not allow. And she wanted a new career as a Certified Nursing Assistant. So, she made her vision board.

She took a home healthcare magazine and saw the abbreviation CNA and put that on her vision board. Then she saw the word *weekly* and put that on the board, next to the dollar amount she wanted to make each week. These three things were separate and not touching.

Now she was feeling a bit more creative…or maybe she was just tired. She took a house she saw online and printed it out. Then she glued a picture of a litter of cats over the house, as she could not find a picture of just one or two cats. She cut out a picture of a car she liked, but could only find a picture of that special vehicle motoring down a busy highway with many other cars also in the picture. She overlapped that car picture with the house and the cats.

What happened? She got her CNA job and the salary she wanted. A realtor found her the perfect house. However, it was on a major highway, just like the picture of the car she wanted that was overlapping the house on her vision board. The house had a bad cat smell too, on account of all the cats the former owners left behind without a litter box. The CNA and salary pictures were not overlapping, and my friend got what she wanted on those fronts. The message here is to be careful with your product placement, so to speak.

Add Your Intention

As you are adhering your words and pictures to your board, do it with intention. Don't start looking at the clock or texting your friends in between. This should be alone time and a time for you to concentrate. As you attach each item or piece of paper, think about how it will feel when you actually have that wish or goal in your life.

Display It!

Finally, put your vision board somewhere you can see it every day so you can remind yourself and the universe of your intentions.

Designing an "I Don't Have a Clue" Vision Board

Before we talk about visualization techniques, there is another vision board method to consider.

The classic vision board I just described is perfect for those of you who know what you want, where you want to go, and what you want to accomplish. But what if you don't know what you want? Maybe you are still searching, experimenting, and trying to figure out your life. You can still make a vision board!

This is what I call an "I don't have a clue" vision board. Many people choose this method, and it's not a cop-out at all. Actually, this exercise can be really enlightening and revealing.

Backing

You should use the same method as the classic design as far as figuring out whether you are using cardboard, paper, a wall with painter's tape, or a corkboard with push pins or thumbtacks.

Pictures and Words

The fun starts with the pictures and the words. Don't think about your future, don't think about a love interest, and don't think about much of anything specific. Just cut out pictures and words or scavenge things like labels or bits of colored or textured paper. Just collect what makes you feel good. Don't analyze it and don't think it could never happen. If it makes you smile and it's positive, use it.

Flipping through magazines works very well. On the Internet you have to search for things in a more specific manner, so it's less useful for this type of board. Magazines and newspapers offer what you don't know you're looking for, if that makes sense.

Chose words that make you happy even if they don't make sense. Maybe just the design of a page or advertisement appeals to you, and you're not sure why. Use it.

Arrange Your Pictures

Like the classic vision board, place your pictures so they are not overlapping. The Eiffel Tower should not have a stack of money in the middle of it, for example, or you may end up being conned into buying the Eiffel Tower. (And just so you know, it's not for sale.)

Add Your Intentions

This requires a "wish-list" mind-set. Sometimes that mentality helps clarify what you really want…and just as importantly, what you don't want (even if you thought you did at one time). It's all right if your vision board looks ill-defined at some points. Just visualizing what you've put there will help you make sense of what direction to move in with your intentions.

Manifesting Your Intentions Using Your Vision Board

Now that you have your vision board all set up…how does this work?

The images you chose are the seeds you've planted that will grow into your future. That's why I believe in creating vision boards during a waxing or full Moon phase. You want to see those seeds blossom into the events, things, and circumstances that you desire.

The moment you finish your vision board, you are giving your brain a command to seek out what you want instead of what you don't want. That's why we don't make negative vision boards of what we don't want, because the universe won't know the difference and might send you more of what you don't want. Only focus on positive outcomes! Saying "I don't want to live in this house anymore" is reinforcing living in that house—and you'll remain there for quite some time to come! Better to phrase it in light of what you do want: "I want a new home with a big yard on a quiet street," and to include a picture of your dream home on your vision board. The universe feels that positive energy and responds in kind. You want to "attract" a positive future that you have specifically chosen.

If you are using the "I don't have a clue" method, you are at least figuring out what you want, and the things on your vision board will start to make sense. Before you know it, you will have a path that is crystal clear to achieving your future dreams.

Making a vision board and letting it sit without taking action is not going to be effective. You can't come back to it every six months and say, "Hey, where the heck is my mansion?" if you haven't taken any steps toward bringing that home into your life.

Visit It Daily

Go to your vision board daily and visualize the things you want on it. Spend at least three minutes doing this. For example, if you want that new car, see yourself driving it, smell those new leather seats, and see the car parked near where you live. If you are looking for a loan, see yourself writing checks to pay your bills. What do the checks look like? How does it make you feel to have that money?

If you have to travel, snap a quick picture of your vision board and take it with you. Don't lose sight of it for too long!

Use the Moon Phases

Use the Moon phases to accentuate your vision. For most things you'll want to use the energy of the full Moon to bring them into your life. If you want to eliminate something, focus your meditation on the waning Moon.

Be Patient

Give the vision board a chance. You have to believe it will work. The more often you have goals that come to fruition, the more you will believe. That's why sometimes it's better to start with smaller things, like a new item of clothing or repairing a certain relationship. Once you bring those things into reality, you'll believe you can manifest the house, the job, and the car.

When your goals do start to come true, leave them on the vision board for a while. You shouldn't remove the picture or thought and say, "One down, five more to go!" The reason is that your first success will help you remember something on your board came true. You may get a little anxious about your goals, even after you've been successful with certain visions or ideas. Being able to see what you've already brought into your life will prevent you from falling into a doubtful state of mind.

Be Grateful

Always be grateful for what you have, and don't focus on what you don't have—this is important.

• • •

Vision boards are a great way to consolidate your goals in one place so you can look at them frequently to remind yourself of where you're headed.

part

3

everyday moon magic

Whether you call them meditations, affirmations, or put a little ritual into it and identify them as spells, Moon magic is all about intention and an appeal to your subconscious. What I present in the following chapters are meditations with a twist. Some forms of meditating are done solely for relaxing and releasing stress. Some meditations generate a vision or messages from the universe or whatever higher power you recognize. We will focus on incorporating the Moon into meditations that will raise your energy level and assist you in directing that energy to create a desired change in your life. Taking into account the various hues of the Moon can be interesting and unique, in addition to lunar eclipses. We will explore meditations related to those phenomena as well as everyday practices that will keep you in balance.

CHAPTER 11

NEW MOON MEDITATIONS FOR NEW BEGINNINGS

The Special Power of New Moon Meditations

The crescent Moon, with that tiny wedge of light, has a lot to offer when you're doing Moon meditations. Some call the new Moon a dark Moon, but there is a difference. A dark Moon is when the Moon is not visible at all. But the moment you can see that crescent is when those new beginnings can take place. It starts to wax in the sky, promoting new developments, activities, and interactions. If you are inside and cannot see the Moon during your meditative time, you can draw one or just envision it.

Sometimes I will go to a window or out the door to get a glimpse and then hold that image in my mind while meditating. Always remember when doing any Moon meditation that your safety and comfort are of primary importance. If you can't be outside, it is not a big deal—you can still get the job done via visualization.

Getting Ready

Note: although I may refer to meditations at night, they can be done in the daytime as well. Energy in the evening is typically quieter, so most people tend to do evening Moon meditations, but it is no less powerful to do these under the light of the Sun.

Prepare Your Setting

Before you begin your meditations:

- Free yourself of any distractions. Shut down those electronics: phones, computers, and tablets.
- Find space where you can be alone. Plan ahead and make sure you are in a place where no one will bother you.
- Try to avoid pets jumping all over you.
- If you like relaxing music, have it in the background. Radio stations with talking don't work.
- Keep your lighting diffused. Candles are okay. (See Chapter 18: Creating a Moon Altar for the meanings of different candle colors or just use some shade of white.)
- Optional: Incense. (Also refer to Chapter 18 for the meanings of different types of incense.)

Prepare Your Mind

Next, it's time to get your mind ready.

- Decide what you are going to meditate on: what is your concern, hope, or aspiration?
- I have provided general meditations for a new Moon that you can use verbatim by filling in the blanks, or you can use them as inspiration to compose your own. If you are going to read from the book, have it next

to you or make a copy of the affirmation you want to repeat. Have these things prepared in advance.

- Put yourself in an altered state of consciousness as discussed in Chapter 7: Learning to Meditate.
- Using your own words, ask your higher power (or whatever you recognize as a universal life force) to permit the Moon's energy to come to you and allow your meditation to be transmitted into the universe and return to you, fulfilling your request. You are sending out a vibration.
- Once you are in that frame of mind, recite out loud or to yourself one of the following meditations.

General Asking Meditation

- Say out loud or to yourself:

"Under this new Moon here tonight, I ask for/that ______________."

- Hold that thought. Close your eyes, visualize it, and reflect on it.
- After you reflect on what you've asked, you need a closing statement to conclude. It can be "Amen," "And so it is," "Blessed be," or anything you feel comfortable with. Sometimes a simple "Thank you" will work. These words may seem very simple, but one concise thought with strong intention and vision is better than hundreds of words without any commitment behind them.

Receiving Messages: Meditation about New Beginnings

During a new Moon, you may not to want to ask for anything, but just listen instead.

- Say out loud or to yourself:

  "Under this new Moon, if there are any positive and valuable divine messages I need to hear, I allow them to come forth."

- Then wait and see if you get a sense of a message. You might think you are making up messages that you want to hear. But take note and be honest. After a while you will know the difference because the real messages may not make sense at first…or they will just feel right.
- After you reflect, say "Amen," "And so it is," "Blessed be," "Thank you," or anything you feel comfortable with.

Finding a New Lifelong Partner Meditation

If you are looking for a partner or mate, the new Moon phase is for you. So many people just want a clean start with someone who they have never met, texted, or found online, or that their friends and relatives haven't already decided they should meet. (You know how it goes: "You have to meet Emma; she would be perfect for you.") You want the universe to find you someone.

(I don't necessarily use the term "soul mate" because I think we all have more than one soul mate out there. It is my personal belief that the universe has a few options for us.) But if you like the word soul mate, go ahead and use it. It's your soul and your mate.

- Recite out loud or to yourself:

  "I give my higher power permission to guide me and bring into my life someone with whom I will have a special connection that will last long-term. I will not give my heart away too early and will take the time to know this individual. Bring him or her into my life and we will start our journey together and see where it takes us. I am patient and I am open to all good people with kind hearts and an understanding of who I am or who I might be."

- After you reflect on what you asked, conclude by saying "Amen," "And so it is," "Blessed be," "Thank you," or anything you feel comfortable with.

New Job or New Business Venture Meditation

This is a good new Moon meditation for those who have never had a job or career, want to quit a workplace, or want to start a brand-new occupation. Note: you do not have to be that specific about a new vocation. If you don't know what to ask for, that's okay. If you do know, profess it in your meditation.

- Recite out loud or to yourself one of the following:

  "At this time in my life I am looking to change my approach to making a living and having a fulfilling and successful career, trade, or business. I want to be/have a __________."

- If you don't know what you want, simply say, "I will be open and excited about the revelation I may have. I understand I may need additional resources, which may include money, partnerships, advice, or connections from others. I will not see failures along the path but only lessons that assist me in going forward. I understand that complaining and looking at what I don't have instead of what will come is unproductive. I am here and ready to see the new opportunities that will come my way. I will not turn down any opportunity, no matter how small, until I contemplate it and take time to embrace it as a gateway to what I am seeking."
- After you reflect on what you asked, conclude by saying "Amen," "And so it is," "Blessed be," "Thank you," or anything you feel comfortable with.

Beginning a New Life Meditation

Finding a new career or love is not the same as starting a new life. Of course, it may tie into those things, but they're not everything. You may have a great line of work or don't have to work at all. Maybe you have the perfect mate or don't want one, and being alone suits you. It could be that being with your pet is just fine. In spite of this, something is missing, and you just don't like where you are in your life now. You desire more.

It's possible that you need a change of place, like a move. Perhaps new friends, or even just one good friend, is what you think you need. Let's say, for whatever the reason, you feel out of sorts. You're just not right. If that is the case, try this meditation to see if you can get yourself back into focus and find happiness using a little Moon magic—a new Moon meditation.

- Recite out loud or to yourself:

  "I sit here before this new Moon with anticipation, because I know my request will be heard. I am on a quest for a new life, whether it is staying where I am at, traveling, meeting others, or taking up new interests. A different state of mind is what I reach out for, which will allow me to be more joyous with what I have. I willingly open my mind to positive discovery of who I am and all the circumstances and people around me that will take me to a place of contentment. I am excited by the fact that although I don't know how it will happen, things will start to shift for me before the next new Moon, and the smiles will come back and the new experiences will be met with enthusiasm."

- After you reflect on what you asked, conclude by saying "Amen," "And so it is," "Blessed be," "Thank you," or anything you feel comfortable with.

• • •

When doing Moon meditations under that new crescent Moon, take into account that all meditations during this phase focus on starting something very original and fresh. The meditations associated with the next phase, the waxing Moon, are more about expanding what you want. It's easy to confuse the two, so be very clear in your own mind about whether your intention is new or an addendum to something you already have started.

CHAPTER 12
WAXING MOON MEDITATIONS FOR AMPLIFICATION OF INTENTIONS

The Power of Waxing Moon Meditations

The waxing stage of the Moon can be considered a waxing crescent, which is barely after a new Moon, when you see only a hint of a crescent. Another waxing phase is when the Moon is half full or better. This phase is technically called a waxing gibbous.

Some people don't do waxing Moon meditations until they see that the Moon is half full or waxing gibbous. There are many people who wait until the Moon is "really" waxing (in the days immediately preceding a half Moon) before they will meditate on an intention. Then again, others think waxing is waxing, and as long as the Moon is getting larger in the sky, it's fine for meditation, be it with the first sign of light or with half or three-quarters illuminated. Honestly, you can do what you feel is best here. It's all about your intent. No one way outshines the other.

Getting Ready

Note: although I may refer to meditations at night, they can be done in the daytime as well. Energy in the evening is typically quieter, so most people tend to do evening Moon meditations, but it is no less powerful to do these under the light of the Sun.

Prepare Your Setting

Before you begin your meditations:

- Free yourself of any distractions. Shut down those electronics: phones, computers, and tablets.
- Find space where you can be alone. Plan ahead and make sure you are in a place where no one will bother you.
- Try to avoid pets jumping all over you.
- If you like relaxing music, have it in the background. Radio stations with talking don't work.
- Keep your lighting diffused. Candles are okay. (See Chapter 18: Creating a Moon Altar for the meanings of different candle colors or just use some shade of white.)
- Optional: Incense. (Also refer to Chapter 18 for the meanings of different types of incense.)

Prepare Your Mind

Next, it's time to get your mind ready.

- Decide what you are going to meditate on: what is your concern, hope, or aspiration?
- I have provided general meditations for a waxing Moon that you can use verbatim by filling in the blanks, or you can use them as inspiration to compose your own. If you are going to read from the book, have it

next to you or make a copy of the affirmation you want to repeat. Have these things prepared in advance.
- Put yourself in an altered state of consciousness as discussed in Chapter 7: Learning to Meditate.
- Using your own words, ask your higher power (or whatever you recognize as a universal life force) to permit the Moon's energy to come to you and allow your meditation to be transmitted into the universe and return to you, fulfilling your request. You are sending out a vibration.
- Once you are in that frame of mind, recite out loud or to yourself one of the following meditations.

All-Purpose Meditation for a Waxing Moon

Whatever phase of the Moon you're meditating under, focus on the power of that phase. Under the waxing Moon, put worries away and focus only on the positive things that you want to increase in your life. In other words, please don't start your meditation by focusing on what you don't want to *lose* (a job, a love, a home). Rather, hone in on what you want to *gain* (a pay raise, a more loving relationship, home improvements). See the difference?

- Recite out loud or to yourself:

> *"I am positioned here in tranquility, allowing the waxing energy of the Moon to embrace me and my desire. That aspiration is…(state your desire). I am grateful for what I have, such as…(state that for which you are grateful, even if it is only one thing). Allow this to come to be."*

- After you reflect on what you asked, conclude by saying "Amen," "And so it is," "Blessed be," "Thank you," or anything you feel comfortable with.

Taking Your Relationship to Another Level

Now, we all know that we can't force another to feel a certain way about us, but how often do we stop to think about how our actions affect our relationships? It's far more possible to move a relationship to another, more intense level if we believe it's going to happen (rather than fearing that it won't). And working out relationship issues is much more likely if we understand our own role in those issues.

- Recite out loud or to yourself:

  "Today I decide to take my relationship to the next step, with the understanding my partner agrees. We will both need patience and acceptance of each other. For this I seek the guidance of my higher power. When I am not being understanding, bring to mind that I should be. When he/she is not understanding, bring to mind that he/she should be. Make us both aware so we can deal with any obstacles along the way. This is what binds two people. We want to be in love, not just love each other."

- After you reflect on what you asked, conclude by saying "Amen," "And so it is," "Blessed be," "Thank you," or anything you feel comfortable with.

Increasing Your Financial Situation

Who among us does not want to improve our finances? But again, take care to frame it in a positive light. Instead of focusing on not having enough to buy a new car, focus on gratitude for what you have right now and think of how having more cash flow will not only better your own life, but the lives of those around you. And be open to knowing that you don't know where a windfall may come from!

- Recite out loud or to yourself:

  "Financial security is nothing to be ashamed of and wanting it is not a selfish yearning. I don't want to yearn; I want to embrace and have. My finances can not only benefit me but others. I will have peace knowing that prosperity is generating toward me. I know it is imminent, and so I wait. I see myself in tune with the universal life force energy, which will allow me to understand opportunities and grasp them. I will wait, but that wait will be before the next waxing Moon, when I will begin to see a process that will take me to the next stage of financial awareness and enable me to take action and make transformations. I will look at all invitations, prospects, and avenues to guide me to the next level of affluence."

- After you reflect on what you asked, conclude by saying "Amen," "And so it is," "Blessed be," "Thank you," or anything you feel comfortable with.

Better Health or Sustaining Good Health

Whether young or old, we may not think about it every day, but our good health is the greatest gift the universe can bestow upon us. People joke when we are down and out about relationships, money, living conditions, and so forth by saying, "At least you have your health." It might not seem comforting at the time, but it is so very true. Whether you have good health or want better health, a meditation under a waxing Moon is something priceless. And since the Moon is free, it literally is priceless!

- Recite out loud or to yourself:

  "Right now in my life there are many things I long for, but without my good health, they will have little meaning. As this Moon, so brilliant in the sky, gets brighter and brighter, I ask for my mental and physical body to become stronger and healthier. Grant that my body may be in a state of positive circumstances, and let it remain so. Allow my body, including my mind (which has some challenges), to become healed, full of life, and restored to an improved condition. Completely renewed will be my goal, and for this, I am motivated to take the initiative to seize opportunities, new ideas, and methods that will bring me into this dwelling of healthiness."

- After you reflect on what you asked, conclude by saying "Amen," "And so it is," "Blessed be," "Thank you," or anything you feel comfortable with.

• • •

As with all meditations, keep it simple and sincere. Know what you're asking for and believe that it can come to pass. Prepare to receive it, and it shall be yours!

CHAPTER 13

FULL MOON MEDITATIONS FOR INTUITION

The Power of Full Moon Meditations

In Chapter 5, we talked about the best time for practicing Moon magic, including how to determine if you are Moon sensitive (open to absorbing negative energy during the full Moon) or Moon tolerant (someone who lets negative energy slide off her back). You may want to review that section prior to practicing the meditations discussed in this chapter, just so you're in tune with your own energy prior to basking in the glow of the meditative Moon.

Full Moon meditations can be done:

- One day before the full Moon
- On the very night of a full Moon
- The day after

The Moon is illuminated approximately 98 percent on these days. Therefore, you have the opportunity to do three full Moon meditations on three separate occasions in a month. The actual full Moon, at 100 percent brightness, only lasts for a minute!

General Full Moon Meditation

When it comes to a full Moon meditation, the vibration is so strong that it is wide open to any type of meditation if you are not Moon sensitive. Therefore, I have included a general full Moon meditation that allows you to fill in your request. Always remain positive and do not do meditation that would have negative consequences for yourself, anyone else, or anything.

- Recite out loud or to yourself:

  "This full Moon energy is something I am here to channel. Come forth and hear my thoughts and wishes. Those wishes will become reality. By the next full Moon, I will start to see the passageway that brings me to my intention. My intention is to.... (state your desire)."

- After you reflect on what you asked, conclude by saying "Amen," "And so it is," "Blessed be," "Thank you," or anything you feel comfortable with.

Meditation for Increasing Psychic Abilities/Intuition

Being psychic or intuitive is something that needs to be developed on a regular basis. It's like a muscle. The more you use it, the stronger it becomes. If you feel limited by the physical world when it comes to finding answers and want to trust your instincts more often, this is something you should consider.

- Recite out loud or to yourself:

  "I have made the decision to allow my psychic abilities to expand and mature. I will use my intuition with a positive attitude for good alone. My psychic aptitude may be much more than I realize. I am open to the vibrations of this full Moon to allow me to concentrate and follow my sixth sense. I also allow any form of divination to assist me in bringing this vibration forward. If I choose not to use any form of divination, I will allow the messages from my higher power to emerge."

- After you reflect on what you asked, conclude by saying "Amen," "And so it is," "Blessed be," "Thank you," or anything you feel comfortable with.

Divination During a Full Moon

The full Moon is also a good time to practice different forms of divination, which, roughly put, is fortune-telling using some type of tools for concentration, like tea leaves or cards, etc. Many of us find that our intuition is increased at the time of a full Moon. There's no way to quantify that; we just feel it. Meditating on the night of a full Moon is very powerful for those who want to increase their ability to predict future events and see beyond the physical realm.

Harness that lunar energy to work with you!

Although doing "readings" of any kind at a full Moon sounds like a recipe for success, this power can be too much for those who are Moon sensitive (see Chapter 5). If this describes you, your level of concentration may become too strenuous and actually block your focus. (I had a friend who always opted to do her readings at a waxing Moon instead of a full Moon for this reason. She explained that she got so excited about the Moon being full, she simply could not bring her thoughts together.) Also, some people who are just starting out with sharpening their intuition lack confidence and feel pressured to perform, which can also lead to a mental Moon block.

On the night or day of a full Moon, I suggest you try some form of divination. Do the suggested meditation I provided for increased intuition earlier in this chapter beforehand to boost your ability to connect with the universe.

Reading Tea Leaves and Coffee Grounds

One example of a simple divination technique is reading tea leaves or coffee grounds. The practice of seeking divine knowledge through the use of interpretive tools and rituals has been utilized by oracles and spiritual masters since before the discovery of tea in Southeast Asia almost 5,000 years ago. In one such system, thought to be the precursor to tea leaf reading, Chinese monks studied the cracks and residue created inside the heart of a bell to understand its message or guidance for restoring health and harmony. This made sense to the monks because the resonance of a bell ringing or chiming was considered a sacred sound, a blessing, believed to ward off evil spirits or negative forces, as well as a method of rebalancing energy. Analyzing the designs of fissures and dirt, leaves, and other debris formed by the bell's vibration was a way of understanding a challenging situation, guiding next moves, and predicting what was coming in the future.

With the birthplace of tea said to be in southwestern China around 2737 B.C., it was most likely the Chinese who first noticed the similarities between a bell and a teacup and started interpreting the residue of tea leaves just as they had the residue inside of bells. Through the centuries, as the popularity of tea traveled from Southeast Asia to Japan, Russia, the Middle East, Europe, and the British Isles, so did the art of what is now known as tasseomancy or tasseography (Arabic *tassa* for cup and *mancy* for divination).

Getting Mentally Prepared

As with all divination, sacred regard and focused intention are vital aspects of the practice of tasseography. It is important to honor and align with the universe and to affirm that for every question, there is an answer; for every problem, a solution. Additionally, it is important to pay attention, remain open, and trust you will easily intuit and understand the guidance provided.

Preparing Your Materials

This is an activity you can do with someone else on the night or day of a full Moon. Some people prefer to read for someone else and then allow that person to read for them. There's less of a chance of you inserting your own subconscious thoughts into a reading that way.

Whether you do this alone or with a friend, have everything prepared in advance. Running back and forth can limit your concentration.

Find the Right Cup

Select a teacup with a handle that is shallow, wide, and white (or light in color) without patterns or designs on the inside (fancy outsides are acceptable). Make sure the teacup has a matching saucer (if possible) and both are made of an earthen material, such as porcelain or stoneware. No mugs. No plastic or Corelle. And absolutely no broken, chipped, or cracked teacups or saucers. Divination tools must be sound, whole, and in good condition to facilitate an empowered connection and a meaningful reading.

Preparing Coffee

You'll need to use whole-bean, coarse-ground coffee in order to produce the type of grounds that will create large, discernible images. Pick a whole-bean blend you like (decaffeinated is okay) and use an in-store or at-home grinder set to a coarse grinding gauge. Do not use instant coffee, single-serving pods, or drip coffeemakers. Use the following steps to prepare your cup of coffee:

1. Lightly boil enough water in a pot for the amount of coffee you want to produce.
2. Measure your coarse-ground, whole-bean coffee. Approximately 1 teaspoon of grounds for every 6 ounces of water works well.
3. Heat the grounds in a small pot on the stove for only a few minutes once the water is boiling.
4. Pour the unfiltered coffee into your cup.
5. Allow your coffee grounds to settle to the bottom of the cup. If you can see the coffee is too clear or looks diluted, there may be a scarcity of grounds for some reason, so sprinkle some more into the cup.
6. Add cream and sugar if this is how you like to drink your coffee. It will not influence the reading.
7. If you had to add any more grounds, stir, stir, stir the mixture for a few seconds to kick up some energy. This will churn the grounds and infuse some vitality. Then let the grounds settle to the bottom.

Selecting and Brewing Tea

Choose any variety of tea you like, just make sure it's loose tea. No tea bags allowed, as the tea is ground too fine; and no tea strainers either. Again, decaffeinated is acceptable and will not produce a weaker reading.

The following is a simple method for brewing a single cup of tea:

1. Measure a little more than 1 cup of fresh, cold, nondistilled water. Spring water and filtered water are good choices.
2. Put the water on the stove to boil in a tea kettle or a saucepan.
3. Place approximately 1 teaspoon of tea leaves in your teacup.
4. The moment the water begins to boil, pour the boiling water over your tea leaves.
5. Steep the tea for 3 to 5 minutes, according to how strong you like your tea.
6. Add a small amount of cream and sugar if you like. It will not affect the reading.
7. Stir the tea and let the leaves settle.

Writing the Message

Before you can read the tea leaves or coffee grounds, you need to "write" the message. The "reader" or "seer" is the person reading the leaves or grounds for the "sitter," the person receiving the reading. The sitter should think about a question or focus on a specific intention while enjoying their cup of tea or coffee according to the following steps:

1. Drink nearly all of the tea or coffee, leaving only a few drops of liquid in the bottom of cup.
2. With the left hand, the sitter holds the cup by the handle, with the rim up.
3. The sitter then swishes the last of the tea or coffee quickly in a circular clockwise motion three times. This distributes the leaves or grounds around the cup.
4. The sitter then turns the cup upside down on the saucer, allowing the remaining liquid to drain naturally. Do not tap on the cup.
5. After the liquid is drained, turn the cup back over. The leaves or grounds should have clumped, forming the shapes that will be interpreted.

If you're reading for yourself, follow the same steps. However, in this case it's important to be honest with yourself about what you see. This is why people often prefer not to read for themselves.

Reading the Message

As the reader, take the cup and prepare to examine its contents. Relax by taking a few deep breaths. At first, looking at all the images can be puzzling. You may not even spot anything that you think resembles any of the likenesses listed later in this chapter.

Translating symbols into a meaningful narrative is highly subjective. Different mental states also contribute to the outcome of the reading. Therefore, as you gaze into the cup, remain relaxed and open; don't become tense. Just allow the patterns to reveal themselves and tell you what or who they represent. You'll hear your inner voice say, "I'm a spider. I'm a circle. I'm a tree."

You'll want to organize your reading by beginning at the handle and moving in a clockwise direction as you turn the cup. The handle should be on the bottom middle, facing the person who is doing the reading, whether that is yourself or someone else.

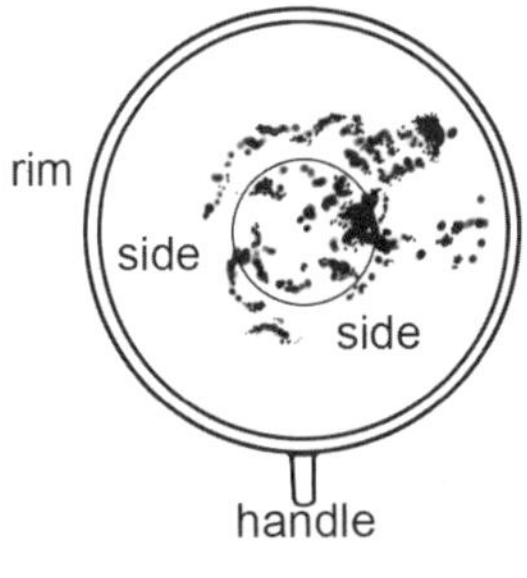

Sample tea leaves reading.

Past, Present, Future

There are some different theories about which area of the cup corresponds with the past, present, and future. It is my experience that this three-part method is the least complicated and the most accurate:

- Rim—Events in the present.
- Sides—Events in the near future (up to three months).
- Bottom—Events further out (up to nine months).

Another method suggests that formations to the left of the handle are things of the past and configurations to the right of the handle are matters relating to the future. The symbols closest to (or immediately to the left or right of) the handle are the present.

Interpreting What You See

Before you start your interpretations, you may want to make a note of what full Moon month the reading is taking place in to see if your "readings" or interpretations are better at some times more than others. For example, jot down or make a file folder on your computer about how accurate your tea leaf or coffee ground reading was under a particular full Moon month compared to other months. You may have been very precise on the full Moon in September—the Harvest Moon—as opposed to the full Moon in November, the Snow Moon. If your connection is better at a specific time, you may have an affinity or better concentration for those months, as your personal energy connects to that month with more passion. Sometimes individuals "read" better in the month they were born in or during times that hold a special meaning. You won't know unless you experiment. Learning is trying out different approaches!

Foremost in interpreting tea leaves or coffee grounds is connecting with and listening to your intuitive self. Your intuitive or wiser self is a master of identifying patterns that will be relevant and have meaning in response to the question posed. It will guide the sitter to greater understanding and insight into the topic and movements of energy that are operating in the given situation. This is more advanced and multidimensional than looking up the meaning of a symbol in a book. Your intuitive self is well equipped to accomplish this if you allow yourself to be guided, listen, and trust the information you are given.

When determining what a formation symbolizes, usually the first thought that comes to mind is the wise choice. Often a shape may appear to have several possible interpretations. In this case, it's best not to overthink it and to go with your initial impression. If you are unsure, keep turning the cup and focusing. Take your time; eventually you'll hear a clear message and come to a deep, resonant understanding. If others are present, their input can be distracting and does not count. You are the designated seer, and your perspective is the only one that matters.

General Shapes

Often the easiest symbols to translate are the symbol designs and geometric shapes. So if a circle or square pops out at you right away, focus on that image and proceed from there. Even if you need to pass over some of the other images at first, that's okay. You are learning, so don't push yourself to do anything 100 percent according to directions. You will eventually find your own way.

Here are the interpretations of basic shapes:

- **CIRCLE**—Success and fulfillment.
- **SQUARE**—Challenge or stability.
- **TRIANGLE**—Good fortune and blessings.
- **STRAIGHT LINE**—Journey or new enterprise.
- **BROKEN LINE**—Something that won't last or a challenging trip.
- **WAVY LINE**—Indecisive travel plans, changes, or water.

Letters or Numbers

When it comes to seeing letters, these can be the letters of someone's first name—especially if your question has to do with people. Or it could be the first initial of a place, such as *A* for Alaska or Asia.

For numbers, it could be a sign of time: 2 could be 2 days, hours, months, or years. The person reading should make that judgment with their gut feeling or whatever their intuition says.

The following are general, positive, and negative meanings. It will be up to you, the "reader," to decipher how you feel when you see the number.

1—General Meaning: Good times in the near future.

- Positive: Individual, active, original.
- Negative: Lazy, unstable, egotistical.

2—General Meaning: An event will soon bring you happiness.

- Positive: Charming, favors partnership, gentle.
- Negative: Dishonest, favors duality, two-faced.

3—General Meaning: Your wish will come true.

- Positive: Abundant, creative, humorous.
- Negative: Jealous, shallow, extravagant.

4—General Meaning: You will enjoy success regarding education.

- Positive: Diverse, adventuresome, unattached.
- Negative: Vulgar, stern, boring.

5—General Meaning: A startling occurrence will shock you.

- Positive: Loyal, stable, conservative.
- Negative: Oversexed, undependable, overindulgent.

6—General Meaning: You will be well liked and popular.

- Positive: Loving, artistic, balanced.
- Negative: Stubborn, dominant, skeptical.

7—General Meaning: Love is coming your way.

- Positive: Scientific, intelligent, trustworthy.
- Negative: Selfish, meddlesome, stubborn.

8—General Meaning: Learning from experience is powerful.

- Positive: Successful, powerful, is a strong leader.
- Negative: Impatient, wastes energy, resentful.

9—General Meaning: Better times are ahead, with dreams fulfilled.

- Positive: Romantic, spiritual, generous.
- Negative: Overemotional, bitter, improper.

Note: a zero is read as a circle, not a number.

Symbols

The following interpretations of symbols are the most important part of tea leaf reading. Although with time and practice you may develop your own impressions, these are the most common and proven interpretations by seasoned readers. Use your first impression and stick with it. Allow your intuitive self to take over. After a while you will learn to trust your initial thoughts.

- *Acorn*—Success is in store for you.
- *Anchor*—Your worries will soon be lifted.
- *Angel*—Expect good news, especially in love.
- *Apple*—Prosperity is coming through business.
- *Arrow*—Bad news is coming your way in matters of love.
- *Baby*—This indicates a series of minor but unfortunate events that will bring about positive change, or it can literally mean a new birth.
- *Bear*—Delays regarding travel will be annoying.
- *Bell*—You will receive good news. More than one bell indicates a wedding.
- *Bird*—You will receive joyous news. Birds flying means news will come quickly.
- *Boat*—A friend will pay you a visit.
- *Book (Open)*—A new lover or new ideas are favorable.

- *Bottle*—Illness is coming your way but can be avoided.
- *Camel*—You will receive unexpected news regarding someone's past.
- *Candle*—Assistance from others will bring you joy.
- *Cat*—Beware of cruelty, enemies, and quarrels.
- *Church*—A ceremony will take place.
- *Clover*—You will have good luck and fortune for a long time to come.
- *Cross*—You will make a sacrifice for someone you love.
- *Crown*—A wish will be granted.
- *Cup*—Success surrounds you.
- *Dagger*—Do not be too hasty. Use caution.
- *Dog*—You have many loyal friends.
- *Door*—This indicates a visitor from the "other side." Also means past knowledge.
- *Dragon*—Changes will happen suddenly for you.
- *Drum*—This indicates a trip due to a new work situation.
- *Ear*—A new lover or new ideas are favorable.
- *Envelope*—You will receive news that will make you smile.
- *Eye*—If you are having difficulties, you will overcome them.
- *Fan*—Some type of flirtation is going on in your life.
- *Flag*—Beware of danger or quarreling.
- *Flower*—You will have much interest in having a new partnership, marriage, or will be receiving compliments from friends.
- *Foot*—You need to take a stand and make a decision.
- *Fork*—Someone you think is a friend isn't.
- *Gate*—It's time to move forward. You will not meet with trouble.
- *Gondola*—This indicates a love affair near the water or at sea.
- *Grasshopper*—News will come to you of someone in the armed forces.
- *Gun*—Conflict is coming into your life.
- *Hammer*—You will have to do work you don't like.
- *Harp*—This indicates a serious love affair.
- *Hat*—You will be presented with a gift or a raise in salary.
- *Heart*—This is a good omen of happiness and pleasure.

- *Horseshoe*—You will be the epitome of the word lucky.
- *Hourglass*—Stop procrastinating and make a decision.
- *House*—You will have security. Things are in good order.
- *Iceberg*—Be cautious with whom you share opinions.
- *Insect*—Your problems are smaller than you think.
- *Jewels*—You will receive a gift or give one to someone else.
- *Jug*—You will enjoy good health, for some time to come.
- *Key*—You will change jobs or careers.
- *Kite*—Dreams will come true.
- *Knife*—This indicates separation from friends or a loved one.
- *Ladder*—Your lifestyle will be elevated for the better.
- *Lamp*—Financial gain is coming your way.
- *Leaf*—A new and better life will befall you.
- *Lightning bolt*—You will encounter negative energy from others.
- *Lock*—There is a great stress on you.
- *Monkey*—Beware of scandal. Don't embarrass yourself.
- *Moon (Crescent)*—Fortune and prosperity are on the rise.
- *Mountain*—You will enjoy achievement, but with numerous difficulties.
- *Mushroom*— You will encounter minor business obstacles.
- *Necklace*—Many admirers will come your way.
- *Needle*—You will be admired for an achievement.
- *Net*—Someone may try to trap you at something.
- *Oar*—You have troubles at home, but things will be amiably resolved.
- *Octopus*—Others may be keeping things from you—danger.
- *Owl*—You will hear good news if this is near the cup's rim. If not—scandal.
- *Palm tree*—You will take a trip to a tropical area.
- *Person*—Someone will unexpectedly come to visit.
- *Pig*—Be careful of being greedy, or of someone else's greed.
- *Pipe*—You are thinking of a man. Other symbols nearby will tell you what he's thinking. Letters nearby could indicate a name.
- *Plane*—A journey awaits you.
- *Question mark*—Morals and motives are questionable.

- *Rabbit*—There will be a need for bravery.
- *Rat*—Someone is dishonest, a possible enemy.
- *Rose*—New friendships and popularity are in store.
- *Shark*—Possible bankruptcy may occur.
- *Shoe*—Your energy level will elevate. You will experience new ventures.
- *Snake*—This is a bad omen. Be careful to avoid trouble.
- *Spider*—You will receive gifts or compensation for a job well done.
- *Star*—All things are good—happiness, health, finances, and love.
- *Teapot*—Many friends will visit you.
- *Telephone*—Remember to do or tell someone something.
- *Thimble*—Changes will happen in the home.
- *Tree*—This indicates recovery from mental or physical ill health.
- *Turtle*—Criticism proves helpful.
- *Umbrella*—This indicates annoying people, places, and things.
- *Unicorn*—This points to a marriage or relationship no one knows about.
- *Vase*—A friend is in need of your help.
- *Vehicles*—This indicates travel or a move.
- *Volcano*—Someone is overemotional—it could be you!
- *Wheel*—Something will be completed or fulfilled.
- *Wings*—Messages will be arriving soon.
- *Witch*—Bizarre circumstances will arise—something peculiar.

Sample Readings

When you have determined what objects you see in the cup, try to make a story out of it. Whether you are doing a general reading or answering a specific question, it is fairly simple to put together a scene.

This is where you need to use your intuition. Simply put, say what your gut feeling is telling you. Another reader could interpret the same formations totally differently. Don't be concerned about being right or what someone else would do.

The following are four examples of how I personally might interpret the exact same symbols in different circumstances.

The symbols in the cup are:

- **ANCHOR**—Your worries will soon be lifted.
- **BIRDS FLYING**—News will come quickly.
- **FLAG**—Beware of danger or quarreling.
- **NEEDLE**—You will be admired for an achievement.
- **NUMBER SEVEN**—Love is coming your way. Or the number 7 literally.

The following are several possible interpretations of those images:

1. **GENERAL READING, INTERPRETATION 1:** Within seven days, you will be admired for staying out of an argument. As a result, present negativity in your life will be removed quickly. By walking away, you will have avoided a dangerous situation.
2. **GENERAL READING, INTERPRETATION 2:** I feel there is a strong indication that you will argue with someone, but the quarrel will end quickly. You will both feel a sense of relief that the air has been cleared. People will agree with you that you were right to end the confrontation before it got worse. The number seven appears in the cup. This tells me it could take place around seven o'clock in the morning or evening. The other possibility is that the conflict could be resolved in seven minutes.
3. Specific question: "Will I find a boyfriend soon?"
    1. **ANSWER 1:** Someone is going to come into your life quickly. Unfortunately, you may find that he has qualities you do not care for, and you may break off the relationship. Others will admire you for your judgment and foresight.
    2. **ANSWER 2:** In approximately seven days, news will come that a guy you know has broken up with his girlfriend. This is due to a quarrel or disagreement. Be careful that you don't get romantically involved too fast. You may be overanxious and wanting to

feel that your loneliness has ended. He will admire you for your caution about relationships. However, I sense much negativity around this whole situation. Other people out there may be more suited for you. If you give him a pass, someone will move into your life soon.

You can understand how these scenarios can be altered. As I mentioned earlier, for this reason, many people cannot read tea leaves for themselves. It is very easy to see what we want to see!

• • •

The full Moon can infuse you with whatever you are looking for, whether that is an achievement, intuition, or a fulfilled request. It's up to you how and if you want to use this phase. The full Moon is Moon magic at it's most excellent, so endeavor to test your sensitivity and see if you are a good match.

CHAPTER 14
WANING MOON MEDITATIONS FOR LETTING GO AND MOVING ON

The Power of Waning Moon Meditations

This Moon phase is a time to release, banish, remove, or reduce. If there is something or someone you want less of, this is the time to take charge and make a change. Many people believe the most powerful time of a waning Moon is when it's decreasing from a half Moon.

Change isn't bad; it's resistance to change that can slow you down. So say goodbye to the unenthusiastic thoughts, the depressing emotions, and the downbeat people. Say goodbye to ill health, extra weight, addictions, and fear. This is a popular Moon phase as many of us have much to get rid of in order to start fresh!

Remember that when you do a releasing meditation, you are not instantly "cured." (Although I do know many people who were able to let go that easily.) Take baby steps and be appreciative of doing this meditation in the first place, because you are making an effort, while keeping in mind that it might take several rounds of waning Moon meditations to be successful.

Yoda, a Star Wars character who is a teacher and philosopher of sorts, says, "Do or do not. There is no try," which is to say, if you're going to do something, then darn it, do it! No wishy-washy, middle-of-the-road thoughts or actions. If you want to part ways with something from the past that is harming you emotionally or even physically, make your decision, focus on this during your meditations, and let go of it in peace, knowing that whatever it is, it has taught you something.

But wait. What about the dark Moon, when there is no visible light in the sky? I think of it as a time to rest and just be. Therefore, I have included one general dark Moon meditation that will speak to this time when it's okay to be still.

General Releasing Meditation for the Waning Moon

Decide what you are going to meditate on: what is it you want to get rid of in your life?

- Recite out loud or to yourself:

  "As the Moon above me wanes, I release these things in my life...(state what or who you want to release). I want these things to no longer be a part of who I am or what I aspire to be. As of this moment, I choose to make this change in my life. As you, my higher power, are my observer, I give you permission to support me in this endeavor. Give me the courage to continue forward if I am not successful immediately. I know I do not always have all the answers I need, so I also release the want or desire to have the solutions. I allow the universe to give me guidance and resolve."

- After you reflect on what you asked, conclude by saying "Amen," "And so it is," "Blessed be," "Thank you," or anything you feel comfortable with.

Waning Moon Meditation for a Breakup

Leaving someone or having someone leave you is never easy. Your thoughts go to that person frequently, and your energy can be drawn in all kinds of different (and not necessarily positive) directions. So, get rid of all those downbeat sensations and let them wane with the Moon. If you are trying to overcome a relationship, use your lunar power. You will most likely need all the advantages you can rally. Let it take the pressure off you.

- Recite out loud or to yourself:

  "As I sit here, I understand that sometimes people come into our lives to teach us lessons and then we must refocus. The reason for the breakup of this relationship is not going to be a concern to me anymore. I will not let depression, anger, or guilt be a part of my being. I will be liberated when these feeling no longer exist. Everyday as the Moon wanes is a day closer I get to having a better understanding of this situation. Even if I don't get "closure," I will not need it. I know someday all will be clear. Help me overcome any situation that brings me to a place of sorrow. For I am filled with hope and excitement to see what my new future has to offer."

- After you reflect on what you asked, conclude by saying "Amen," "And so it is," "Blessed be," "Thank you," or anything you feel comfortable with.

Waning Moon Meditation for Discharging Poor Health

Whether young or old, the superstar in your life is your health. It should always be front stage and center. So get rid of those players that do you no good and start a new performance!

- Recite out loud or to yourself:

    "The waning Moon has beckoned me to use its power to help me expel my health issues. Those health issue are...(state your health issues, whether physical or mental). I ask to be free of this state of health, and I am open to a healing energy that will encompass me after this condition is resolved. I maintain an open heart and have faith and belief that your divine assistance will encompass me."

- After you reflect on what you asked, conclude by saying "Amen," "And so it is," "Blessed be," "Thank you," or anything you feel comfortable with.

General Dark Moon Meditation

I feel a dark Moon is suited for being at peace and contemplating things from your past that you are grateful are gone or that are going away. It's also a good time to gently plan the directions you want to go in life.

Some like to do waning meditations, such as those related to getting rid of addictions, on the night of a dark Moon. But in my opinion, relaxation and reflection are the ideal choice. There is no visible light in the sky, and that indicates a period of quiet and void.

- Recite out loud or to yourself:

  "Tonight I am taking this time for reflection. I also acknowledge and thank the resources I have known as my higher power…(state who they are or just leave it as "higher power"). I am appreciative of the things I have had the courage to erase that were holding me back from accomplishments."

- After you reflect on what you asked, conclude by saying "Amen," "And so it is," "Blessed be," "Thank you," or anything you feel comfortable with.

• • •

When you release something from your mind, it gives you the grounding you need to start a new chapter. Don't forget about your past, but don't dwell on it. The "I don't know what I was thinking" and the "I can't believe I was doing that" thoughts are okay for a while. But after that, you have to let go of past mistakes and look to what you can do better in the present and future. And that's what the waning Moon is all about—letting go.

CHAPTER 15

BLUE MOONS, RED MOONS, AND ECLIPSES

Unique Lunar Events

You've learned all about the regular lunar phases at this point, but what about those other Moons you hear about periodically? These Moon events cry out and say, "Take notice!" whether through their brightness, quirky names, or even reference in local news stories. Some of the names you may be familiar with, and others…not so much. Let us explore these events so you have a better understanding of what they are, why they happen, and how you can harness their energy in your own life.

These unique lunar events are as follows:

- Supermoon
- Mini Moon
- Blue Moon
- Black Moon
- Blood-Red Moon
- Ring of Fire Eclipse

Mark your calendar when these events are going to occur. If not, you might wait all year for the Supermoon or mini Moon and sleep through it!

Please, my dear readers, remember I am not a scientist or an astronomer, so everything presented here is in layman's terms—not just for your sake, but for mine too!

Supermoon

A Supermoon occurs when a full or new Moon coincides with the Moon's closest approach to the earth. Because it's at the closest point to the earth, the Moon appears larger. In the scientific community, this is called a "perigee-syzygy" Moon. (It's easier to just remember Supermoon, yes?) Syzygy means the direct alignment of three celestial bodies (in this case, Earth, Moon, and Sun). This event happens approximately every 411 days. Thus, roughly every fourteenth full Moon will be a Supermoon, so almost one a year.

Even though Supermoon events have been happening since before early humans turned their eyes to the sky, the term "Supermoon" is new. This now widely known term was originated by astrologist Richard Noelle in 1979 for an article published in *Horoscope* magazine and then popularized by the media during an extremely close approach of a full Moon in March 2011.

Because the full Moons that immediately come in the day before and the day after a Supermoon are still very close to Earth, we see three supersized Moons for three days in a row. Since a full Moon cycle is approximately three days, this translates into three Supermoon meditations, divinations, or contemplations in a row! Nature gives us so many opportunities for free, if we pay attention.

The next time you're planning to observe a Supermoon, remember that it's best viewed after moonrise, when the Moon is just above the horizon. It is then that you'll be able to take full advantage of this Moon illusion, which makes the Moon seem bigger and brighter when compared to the surrounding landscape.

Historically, the Supermoon of November 14, 2016 was the closest since January 26, 1948. The next full Moon that will come as close to the earth will take place on November 25, 2034. The closest full Moon of the twenty-first century will fall on December 6, 2052.

Brightness Effects

As the largest apparent size of the Moon as seen from Earth, a Supermoon looks about 7 percent bigger and about 16 percent brighter than an average full Moon and as much as 14 percent bigger and 30 percent brighter than when the Moon is at its highest point. That's a lot of extra Moon energy!

Scientific Effects

Beyond the visual, there are scientific effects of a Supermoon on our planet. The already powerful lunar tidal effect is intensified by as much as 18 percent due to the Moon 's proximity to the earth. This stronger tidal wave force can cause a two-inch (five-centimeter) variance from regular full and new Moon tides.

While some astrologers have suggested that Supermoon events are responsible for natural disasters, such as volcanic eruptions, earthquakes, tsunamis, and hurricanes, there is no scientific evidence that supports a link between a Supermoon and catastrophes of this kind. However, scientists do attribute some increase in the movement of the large plates of rocks (tectonic plates) that make up the earth's crust, which amplifies tidal activity during a Supermoon.

How to Harness the Energy of a Supermoon

What a time to catch fish! Romantic situations during this phase? To put it tastefully, they can be stimulating and more intense than routine.

The unparalleled nighttime illumination of a Supermoon is also said to offer enlightenment regarding unrealized aspects of our souls and provide access and insights into unexplored emotions and alternative life paths. Energies are typically magnified, emotions amplified, and expressions intensified during full and Supermoons. Feelings tend to flow more freely, events and incidences are experienced more profoundly, and drama is often heightened. Drive for change is fortified, new beginnings take on a more meaningful quality, and conclusions and realizations seem even more climactic. If you want to do a meditation on the night of a Supermoon, refer to the meditations that are appropriate for full Moons or new Moons, depending on what phase it is for that particular Supermoon, keeping in mind Supermoons only occur on a full or new Moon phase.

Supermoons always remind me of a friend's thirtysomething-year-old brother who never seemed to know what he wanted to do in life. Nothing seemed to appeal to him, so he worked at a bait shop because he enjoyed fishing, and it was something he understood at least. Being a commercial fisherman was out as he didn't care for the business. He just liked to fish. (I might also mention he wasn't very motivated.) I'm not saying he was lazy… just not very enthusiastic about anything. Okay, he was lazy.

His sister (my friend) believed in the magic of the Moon and doing meditations for what she wanted in life. Of course, since it required effort, he had no interest. He believed somewhat but didn't want to go the extra step to even try anything like meditation. Then it was the night of a Supermoon (of which he was aware). I thought he might go fishing because of the tides, but no. He wasn't in the mood. His sister finally bribed him with the promise that she would wash his truck the next day if he came out with her to do a Moon meditation. She could have done it inside her house, but she wanted to be outside and did not want to go by herself. He finally said yes. He sat with a beer while she did her meditation and was very polite and did not bother her. Then she said, "Why don't you just try?" So he decided to give the Supermoon meditation, that was on a full Moon, a whirl. He concentrated on making money without working very hard and making money while he was not doing anything. Money always coming in somehow, even if he wasn't working. He had nothing really in mind.

Did he believe? He claimed to—in fact, he was so confident that he thought only one meditation should do it. A few weeks later, he was talking to a fellow at the bait shop about a special fishing rod he made to make fishing easier for him. Long story short, the man he talked to tried his fishing rod, had connections to investors, and before he knew it, his product was making him money while he slept. The product is still on the market today, doing well, and this happened years ago. Now that's a super story.

Mini/Micro Moon

So, if there is a Moon that is abnormally large approximately once a year, is there one on the opposite end of the size spectrum? There is. When the full Moon is the farthest distance away from the earth, she's a mini Moon. This also happens yearly. Minis are hard to notice in the night sky. For the most part, mini Moons are undetectable to the unaided human eye—yet dedicated ancient skywatchers developed and employed tools and instruments to measure the Moon's diameter, documenting changes in the size of near and far Moons from month to month. It should be noted that "mini Moons" is also the nomenclature used by NASA to describe small asteroids in Earth's orbit. Therefore, some people prefer the term "Micromoon," but both are used to describe the Moon at its most distant point from Earth.

Brightness Effects

When the Moon is farthest away from Earth, it appears about 8 percent smaller in the sky than an average full Moon. It will also be about 15 percent less luminous.

How to Harness the Energy of a Mini Moon

Mini Moons (although they sound like small chocolate snacks) are good times for beginners to do psychic readings because the energy is a little more gentle and not so intimidating. If you want to do a meditation on the night of a mini Moon, refer to the meditations that are appropriate for full Moons. Try using mini Moons to ask three simple things as opposed to one big one—things that are not life changing but fun. For example: will I get that new bike on sale if I wait another week? Will my ex really switch with me and take the kids for the weekend even though it's not his turn? Will that brunette with the body of Venus at the gym finally talk to me after avoiding me since I joined? Of course, write down your answers so you don't forget.

Better write the questions too!

Blue Moon

The term "blue Moon" has multiple meanings that have evolved throughout history, mostly in the last 400 years. Today, it's an unscientific term that's primarily used as a phrase to describe something that is improbable and rare, as in "once in a blue Moon."

However, it also refers to an extra full Moon that appears in our calendar approximately every two or three years. As we know, most years have twelve full Moons that occur roughly every month. But after a while, there's a bonus full Moon that's called a blue Moon. This happens because the solar calendar has about eleven more days than the lunar calendar. After a few years, those extra days accumulate, and the result is a calendar year that has a thirteenth full Moon.

With the calendrical blue Moon phenomenon having two definitions (the third of four full Moons in a season and also the second full Moon in a particular month), there are differing dates for its most recent and next occurrences.

- With a reoccurrence pattern of approximately thirty-two months and having last experienced a blue Moon as the second full Moon in a month on July 31, 2015, we can look forward to the next showing on January 31, 2018.
- We last experienced a blue Moon as the third of four full Moons in a season on May 21, 2016 and can expect it to come around again on May 18, 2019.

Origins of the Name

Some sources suggest that it's known as a blue Moon because it was named the Betrayer Moon, the outcast that didn't fit into a normal twelve-Moon cycle. In old Middle English, the word for "betrayer" was *belewe*. Over time, it is thought the word evolved into blue.

Philip Hiscock, a folklorist at the Memorial University of Newfoundland, researched and uncovered other blue Moon information dating back to the sixteenth century. His research found the term blue Moon was first used to mean "absurd" and then later in the eighteenth century to be mean "never." Then in the nineteenth century, actual visible blue Moon incidences started to occur and transformed the meaning yet again, to refer to actual blue-colored Moons. Events that prompted this definition included the explosion of the Indonesian volcano Krakatoa in 1883, Indian droughts in 1927, and massive forest fires in Canada in 1951, all of which imparted a blue tinge to the Moon as a result of excessive dust particles being scattered into Earth's atmosphere. With the reality of a verifiable blue Moon becoming a known phenomenon, the well-known and popular phrase "once in a blue Moon" was born.

Hiscock also discovered a calendrical blue Moon reference from 1937 in the now nonexistent *Maine Farmer's Almanac*. This reference was featured in an entry for August. According to Hiscock, the almanac explained that the Moon "usually comes full 12 times in a year, three times for each season. Occasionally, however, there will come a year when there are 13 full Moons, not the usual 12. And that extra full Moon also meant that one of the four seasons would contain four full Moons instead of the usual three."

The definition of the blue Moon as the fourth full Moon in a season would have been derived from early Christian religious calendar calculations that were based on the cycles of the Moon. The year with the extra full Moon distorted the Christian calendar and called for a creative solution (such as labeling the extra full Moon the Betrayer Moon) that allowed for the prescribed observance of church-sanctioned holy day rituals and celebrations. This is one possible explanation for why the extra full Moon might have been labeled *belewe*, or "the betrayer."

Finally we come to the most recent definition of a blue Moon—that of the second full Moon in a single month. Referring again to Hiscock's research, this meaning resulted because of a poor interpretation of the August 1937 *Maine Farmer's Almanac* entry that appeared in a 1946 *Sky & Telescope* article. The misinformation was again reported thirty-four years later in 1980 by a nationally syndicated radio program. Broadcast across the US, the idea of the blue Moon as the second full Moon in one month captured the imagination of listeners and proliferated throughout popular culture. It's now more widely known and accepted than the original Betrayer Moon definition.

How to Harness the Energy of a Blue Moon

Energetically speaking, because blue Moons are just full Moons that occur infrequently, they are thought to be emotionally charged and packing double the energy.

So what can you do on the night of a blue Moon? Seize the moment. Remember, a blue Moon only happens about every 2.5 years, so let's use it wisely!

Blue Moon energy is very intense as it happens so rarely. Since we have twice the force to work with, you might want to meditate on a long-term goal. The reason behind setting long-term goals is that blue Moon energy keeps working until the next blue Moon takes place. (This happens with a regular full Moon as well, but we have more energy to utilize now!)

If, for example, you are looking to have a career in the theater, you plant the seed at this blue Moon for your career to start to move forward. Hopefully in 2.5 years, at the time of the next blue Moon, you will be onstage in a starring role. That's the long-term goal. Maybe you are a chef and your goal is to have your own restaurant by the next blue Moon. If you are a student, you may want to have your career in place by the next blue Moon.

If along the road you change direction…no worries. You won't be "stuck" with your original thought. The universe is used to change, and you are free to change your goal. However, you will have to make that change under a full Moon. The blue Moon energy is only going to be good for that one thought. Let's say you want to be a lawyer and your blue Moon meditation is focused on this. Things are going along quite nicely when suddenly your Aunt Mary invites you to her home in Maine and asks you to work at a plant that produces maple syrup. Hmmmm. You've decided you don't want to be a lawyer anymore. Will the blue Moon energy force you to study law? Of course not. You have just turned directions and have to do something different. So you wait for a dark Moon to contemplate, and then on the night of a waxing Moon, you do your ritual to move to Maine and become a business partner or owner. Nothing is set in stone. Life is all about change.

(And, who knows—you might end being a lawyer for all the maple tree growers in that state.)

Blue Moon Ritual

Whatever the ritual, remember the basic tenets of setting intention: always make it positive, harm none, and no ill intentions to yourself and anyone or anything else. Get into your altered state of consciousness, as set forth in Chapter 7.

Look at the Moon

Sit outside looking at the blue Moon, or in a window or door that faces it if it's raining. If the weather or landscape does not allow this, burn a blue candle and look at it. Don't have a blue candle or don't want to bother looking for one or buying one? Draw a full Moon on a piece of paper and put it in front of you. Improvise. Got a blue plate that's round? Why not?

This can be a ceremony or tradition you follow during every blue Moon. Of course, you can take any of the full Moon meditations from this book and add them to your ceremony.

Set Your Intention

I like this ritual as it doesn't require gathering lots of things. But you will need a pencil and paper. Write down, under the blue Moon (or what you are using for a blue Moon symbol), what you want to achieve as one single goal in the next 2.5 years. You can cheat a little if you stay in the same category. For example, if you want to get married, you might include the place, the home you want to live in, and children if you chose to. You don't want to think, "I want to get married, become a famous scientist, have five homes in Europe, one in Asia, and a condo on the beach in Barbados." That's way too diverse and confusing.

The good news is that blue Moon energy lingers for three days after, so you could do a different ceremony each day. That's like getting three wishes! You can do a different intention on each of these days, but be realistic.

Don't use anything that involves a keyboard to write. Put pen to paper here, people. You are making it so very personal when you write, and your energy is stronger and connects to this natural event better. When you bring in technology, you lose that part of nature that is so important. It's like saying you are going camping and then having a pizza delivered to the campsite. You've cut out part of your connection and work to make the event special. Don't put it on your *Facebook* page or enter it into the realms of social media. You can type it into your computer after you've handwritten it, if you must—just don't use the computer to write the original.

With that said, once you write down what you want, take that paper and put it somewhere you won't lose it. You can make copies if you don't trust yourself. Once you are done writing, focus on your intention. Sit with it and feel the Moon energy as you connect with it. Visualize yourself being successful in your goal and allow yourself to feel that success. Let this be your focus for several minutes. End the session with closing words, as always, like, "Let it be," "Amen," or "And so it is." It seems too simple, but you may be surprised to see how it all transpires.

Black Moon/Dark Moon/Dead Moon

This Moon is the the flip side to the blue Moon. Unfamiliar to many because it is an all-but-invisible Moon phase that has not been nearly as well branded as the blue Moon phenomenon, a black Moon, like its counterpart, has multiple names and meanings.

Some other names associated with a black Moon are Nesting Moon, Birth Moon, Milk Moon, Mother's Moon, Fasting Moon, Courting Moon, Mating Moon, Seed Moon, Journey Moon, Sorting Moon, and Death Moon.

Almost always associated with a new Moon, the following four definitions describe the black Moon phenomenon:

1. As the dark twin to a blue Moon, a black Moon can refer to **THE THIRD NEW MOON IN A SEASON OF FOUR NEW MOONS.** The names for the other three Moons in a season of four are Secret Moon, Finder's Moon, and Spinner Moon. These black Moons occur about once every thirty-three months. The last happened August 21, 2017, and the next will occur August 18, 2020.
2. Again, as with blue Moons, in a more recently constructed modern role, black Moons are also defined as **THE SECOND NEW MOON IN A SINGLE MONTH.** This happens approximately once every twenty-nine months. Because of time zone differences, the month they happen can vary around the globe. The last incidence of this variety of black Moon occurred on October 30, 2016 and can be observed again on July 31, 2019.
3. A third type of black Moon occurs in **A CALENDAR MONTH WITHOUT A NEW MOON.** February is the only month in which there cannot be a new Moon because it is the only month that is shorter (twenty-eight days) than one lunation period (twenty-nine days). This a very rare occurrence, only staged once every twenty years. In this instance, both January and March will have a second new Moon. The last black Moon fitting this definition occurred in 2014 with the next scheduled for 2033. Because of time zone differences, these black Moons may not happen all over the world.

4. The fourth sort of black Moon is defined by **THE ABSENCE OF A FULL MOON IN A CALENDAR MONTH**. As with the absence of a new Moon, this can only happen in February because it is the only month with twenty-eight days. Again, with this type of black Moon, both January and March will have two full Moons. Recurring once approximately every twenty years, the next black Moon meeting this definition will occur in 2018, while the last one was in 1999. Because of time zone differences, these black Moons may not happen all over the world.

On August 21, 2017, a black Moon classified as the third new Moon in a season of four variety caused a total solar eclipse. It was billed as the "Great American Eclipse" because it was potentially visible, depending on weather, coast-to-coast across the US.

Origins of the Name

Recognized by Celtic Druids as a positive influence, the black Moon was considered a time of great opportunity, change, and fortuitousness. Associated with altered states of awareness and higher consciousness that facilitate the acquisition of new knowledge and enhanced wisdom, it is said to illuminate the shadow self and encourage us to embrace weaknesses and realize strengths.

Harnessing the Energy of the Black Moon

Doubling the deep magic of new beginnings and the energy and potential of fresh seed plantings, the new black Moon elicits intuitive qualities, directs intentions, and harnesses spiritual power for soul searching, inner journeys, fortune-telling, and rituals. Believed to herald a period of miracles and fruitful outcomes more intense and powerful than the blue Moon, black Moons reportedly open portals to other dimensions that aid communication and connection with ancestral spirits and ascended masters.

The black Moon is a good time to do meditations for banishing, getting rid of things you don't want in your life, and reflecting. If you like fortune-telling, this is an excellent time for you to take that psychic path. All these are included in the full Moon and dark Moon meditations in Chapters 13 and 14.

Eclipses

Eclipses are astronomical events that occur when one celestial body moves into the shadow of another and is partially or totally shaded. Revering the power of the Sun and the Moon and their influence in our lives, humans have always been captivated by the mystery of eclipses. Lacking a cosmic perspective and an understanding of the larger patterns and dynamic workings of the solar system, early humans created numerous stories to explain the temporary darkening of the Sun or Moon. Rooted in the ancient Greek word for "failure" or "abandonment," we get a sense of the fear and uncertainty early humans often associated with eclipses. It is therefore no wonder people created narratives to make sense of the significance of these unusual, seemingly threatening, and then-unpredictable celestial events. Although, for some more sensitive and advanced souls, eclipses have always opened doors to multidimensional and intergalactic communications and messages.

Over time and through close observation of the shadows cast during eclipses, ancient astronomers eventually figured out that the earth was round and that eclipses were merely shadows cast by other celestial bodies. And even though we've come to understand Earth's place and actions in the larger cosmos and now celebrate these celestial events with road trips and viewing parties, we continue to closely study eclipses in order to expand our knowledge of and relationship with the natural and spiritual world.

Planetary transits and stellar alignments have always been thought to be highly charged with tremendous prophetic power and predictive value. Both lunar and solar eclipses were viewed as a way for otherworldly deities to convey crucial messages to humanity during critical evolutionary moments. Typically eclipse energy was active and honored for a five-day period (two days before and after the day of the eclipse). This time was considered favorable for gaining insights related to advancing humanity's spiritual development and was meant to emphasize the importance of tuning in rather than engaging in mundane activities.

In preparation and response to eclipses, people around the world conjured up demons to blame and creatively imagined and invented solutions to restore balance. They downsized and tamed the unknown, overwhelming, and inexplicable by crafting relatable stories and enacting healing rituals in order to calm anxieties, connect with luminary deities, and open pathways to new levels of consciousness.

What Are Eclipses?

From our perspective on Earth, we experience two types of eclipses: eclipses of the Sun and eclipses of the Moon. These occur when the Sun, Earth, and Moon arrange themselves in a straight or near-straight line. When the new Moon's shadow crosses Earth's surface, we experience a solar eclipse, whereas when the full Moon moves into the shadow of Earth, a lunar eclipse occurs. Within the spectrum of solar and lunar eclipses there are annular and penumbral eclipses. A lunar penumbral eclipse is basically a shadow cast on the Moon by Earth and is significantly less dramatic than a solar annular eclipse. Annular eclipses are similar to total eclipses in that the Moon precisely lines up with the Sun. However, in this eclipse, the Moon is at the point farthest from Earth (called apogee) and is too far away to completely block all light. Thus, the Moon appears too small in the sky to cover the solar disk entirely. Annular eclipses are considered as powerful as other eclipses with effects lasting for up to six months.

All eclipses are a superior time for doing meditations for transformations, like quitting smoking, drinking, or any other addiction. (But don't wait a long time for an eclipse to do it...that's just procrastinating!) You can also do those meditations under a waning or dark Moon. Think of eclipses as a time of change and an opportunity to eliminate chaos from your life.

Total Lunar Eclipse—A Blood-Red Moon

A total lunar eclipse occurs when the Moon moves completely behind the earth's shadow. On average, total lunar eclipses take place nearly once a year.

Nowadays, we understand that because of the way the earth's atmosphere scatters light through dust particles, a total eclipse of the Moon often appears coppery or crimson. (This is similar to what gives a blue Moon its color, though the Moon's exact shade of red depends on the amount of dust in the atmosphere at the time of the eclipse.) When there is a higher quantity of dust particles, the Moon will appear darker red. Despite the fact that the Moon only appears red during some lunar eclipses, there is a tendency to call all total lunar eclipses a blood-red Moon.

People have always counted on the reliability of the Sun and Moon and their movements. To ancient cultures, when the light of either the Sun or the Moon was blocked, it was considered an inauspicious event for the life that depends on it. Seen as a challenge to the normal order of daily life, any darkened, red, or temporarily invisible Sun or Moon would have been an unsettling event. To this day, apocalyptic, end-of-the-world prophecies are still associated with eclipses. Here are some ancient stories of lunar eclipses:

- Ancient Mesopotamians viewed lunar eclipses as an assault on the Moon and translated this to mean an attack on their land and their king. With a fairly reliable ability to predict eclipses, they prepared for them by installing a surrogate king to prevent harm from befalling the true king.
- The Inca believed a lunar eclipse was caused by a jaguar attacking the Moon. As they might do in the case of an actual jaguar attack, they would make loud noises to scare the attacker away, including beating their dogs to make them howl and bark.
- In Korea, it was gigantic hounds attacking the Moon.
- The Vikings explained that sky wolves, or *warg*, chased and ate both the Sun and Moon.

- It was a common belief in Vietnam that a giant frog ate the Sun during a solar eclipse. All this hunting and eating of animals was used to explain the red color of eclipses.
- Some North American natives thought it was the spirits of the dead trying to eat the Sun or Moon while others believed the Moon was sick. In the latter case, tribe members gathered together to sing and chant prayers that restored the Moon back to health.
- One tribe in Africa accounts for eclipses as fights between the Sun and the Moon. Tribe members settle the celestial dispute by offering conflict resolution advice until the eclipse abates.

A "Ring of Fire" Eclipse

One particularly visually interesting type of partial solar eclipse happens when the Moon covers the Sun's center, leaving the Sun's visible outer edges to form a "ring of fire" around the edge.

This is also known as an annular eclipse.

• • •

These unique Moon events are always fun to watch and interact with (if you can do so safely). A combined Supermoon lunar eclipse is scheduled for 2033. That should be interesting!

CHAPTER 16
INCORPORATING THE MOON INTO YOUR DAILY PRACTICES

What Are Your Routines?

Daily routines organize us when it comes to things like showering, walking the dog, practicing yoga, checking emails, and connecting with nature. We have daily routines even if we don't think we do: getting up, eating, and brushing your hair are daily rituals. Some people write down their daily routines and take them very seriously. Others have developed their routines by accident. For instance, they wake up at six thirty every morning because the cat jumps on the bed. It wasn't exactly their intention, but they get used to it, and hence, a daily practice begins. So whether you have taken hours, days, or weeks to figure out a schedule that works to keep you orderly, goal focused, health conscious, and in a joyous frame of mind, or you have simply stumbled upon a routine…your daily practice is already in place.

A Little Morning Moon Magic

Although I know time can be limited in the morning, I have included a few ideas here to help you stay lunar conscious. You can easily incorporate them into your everyday customs—they will only add several minutes to your schedule.

Be Grateful

Being grateful is not a time-consuming exercise because you can do it before getting out of bed with only a couple seconds of thought. Simply think about what you are grateful for. Even the act of awakening is something to be grateful for! When you do Moon meditations, it helps if you are always grateful, so this is a good habit to start.

You don't have to go through a long mental list of things you are thankful for if you prefer not to—that's up to you and the time you have. If you already have a gratefulness habit, keep it going!

Simple Cleansing Rituals

Whenever you wash yourself, you can take an opportunity to do a quick visualization meditation. It's doing a lunar releasing ritual in the privacy of your own home or wherever you are. No matter what the phase of the Moon may be, you need to take showers or wash yourself now and then, so you can't just wait for the Moon to wane before you do this. Therefore, just see in your mind's eye the general light of the Moon surrounding you (white light—keeping it around you till you're done) as you purge yourself from the woes of the day. This can be applied to all the following methods.

Shower Meditation

When you take a shower (whether in the morning or evening), visualize all the negative energy washing down your body and down the drain. If you are not well, see that illness running right out of you onto that shower floor and down the pipes.

Handwashing Meditation

Even if you who don't take a daily shower, you can still take the time to clear yourself of negativity with soap and water. At the very least, when you wash your hands, see all the unhelpful vibes from the day come up from your feet and down from your head into your hands. Then wash, wash, wash, and see that energy going down the drain.

Bathing Meditation

For those of you who only take baths, you might think about a quick shower afterward to fully rinse yourself off. When you get out of the bathtub, give your hands a shake over the tub while the water is draining. Shake that energy off of you! When you are doing Moon meditations, you can also follow this procedure by giving your hands a good shake out in front of you or at your side and send that energy flying, letting it go where it needs to go. Sometimes if I am around someone during the day or night who I think is draining my energy—an energy vampire—I will just shake my hands once I'm away from that person, even if my hands are dry, and see that negative energy moving away from me. Call it a moonshake!

Aquatic Moonlight Cleanse

If you are near a body of water, such as a lake, ocean, or even a swimming pool, you can use that as a cleansing spot as well—not only to wash away the daily grime but also to rid yourself of anything unfavorable that happened throughout the day or night. As you do it, look to the skies. Since the river has no drain and so forth, imagine all the feelings and the physical things you don't want anymore going out to sea far away from you. If you are in a swimming pool, imagine these things are going right straight up and out to the sky, whether your pool is indoors or out.

Vision Boards

If you have a vision board, take a couple of minutes and focus on the board before starting your day. Remember I said earlier that we can't just create the board and do nothing? This is a must for one of your daily practices! So focus on the things you want to bring to fruition—and remember to phrase your wants in a positive manner. For example, instead of saying,

"I don't want to work this dull, dead-end job anymore," phrase it in terms of what you do want, like, "I see myself working in a school with children in a creative capacity."

Do Something Nice for Someone

Do something nice without expecting anything in return. Use the Moon's phases for inspiration. For example, if the Moon is waning, it is a good time to get rid of things, so give someone those extra wine glasses you never use. Or take that extra apple coffee cake over to the neighbor. Buy-one-get-one-free deals at the grocery store aren't always the best for a weight loss program, but it is an opportunity to share with others while removing temptation from the house.

A waxing Moon, a time to grow and expand, means you can expand friendships as well. Ask that new guy at the gym—the one who just moved into your neighborhood—if he is interested in hanging out with you and your buddies someday. The new crescent Moon urges you to email, text, or call someone you have been meaning to get in touch with but never seem to get around to contacting.

During the dark Moon, when there is no visible light in the sky, you can mentally send well wishes to someone you think needs it. Even if you have a long list of twenty people who could use a little boost, you can think, "I am sending positive energy this day to all I know who are in need of contentment." It beats naming each one. The universe knows who you think about and would like to see happy.

Do a Daily Moon Phase Check-In

Check the phase of the Moon daily. A quick look at your Moon phase website or your trusty calendar can set the pace for how your day might transpire. Before you leave your home, think about how the phase of the Moon could affect your to-do list. For example, if the Moon is waning and you have a choice to sign an agreement, I would wait awhile till the Moon is waxing and almost full—a phase that promotes a fair deal for all parties.

By now you know that the Moon has certain energies that can help you bring things into—or send things out of—your life. In this section, we'll talk about some very specific examples of how and when to use the Moon's energy. You can make this part of your regular routine and mark your calendar to remind yourself to tune into the Moon prior to these events. (You'll recall we discussed phases of the Moon as they relate to surgeries and healing in Chapter 6. You can refer back to that chapter for planning purposes as well.)

New Moon

Even though the Moon is dark and all but invisible, this phase marks a time to plant new ideas and renew the outdated. It is a phase of heightened potential and fortuitous new beginnings.

- **BUSINESS GROWTH:** The new Moon is an auspicious time to start a new business, schedule a grand opening, connect with new business contacts, enter into partnerships, or make crucial decisions, because this is when people are open to what is fresh and innovative. This energy continues into the next Moon phase, waxing.
- **INTERVIEWING FOR A JOB OR PROMOTION:** The new Moon is believed to increase confidence, boldness, and chances of success. This is also a good time to join a new club or organization. This energy continues into the next Moon phase, waxing.
- **VACATION/HOLIDAY:** This is a good time to pause and focus on rejuvenation. Avoid taking a holiday during a waning Moon, as it is associated with delays and problems when traveling.
- **MOVING:** It is lucky to move into a new home during a new Moon; prosperity is said to increase as the Moon grows.

- **SHOPPING:** Look for and plan to benefit from amazing bargains during a new Moon. Avoid shopping during the full Moon as this is when we are more likely to impulse buy. During the waning Moon you may find customer service associates are not very helpful and good deals less plentiful.

Waxing Phase

Starting between seven and fourteen days after the new Moon, this phase symbolizes regeneration. With an overabundance of positive energy, it has been shown to be a favorable time for growth, success, courage, luck, health, and friendship. This period is considered the best time to perform tasks that require strength and fertility. It is the ideal time to embark on something new that you want to increase and multiply in your life.

- **ACCELERATE HAIR GROWTH:** Conditions during the waxing Moon promote hair growth and repair after a haircut. Hair care treatments and conditioning rinses are particularly effective in this phase.
- **SURGERY TO AUGMENT:** If you're adding something to your body, such as a pacemaker, a heart valve, a new hip or knee joint, or breast implants, this is the time to do it. It seems this might include tattoos as well. Surgery during a waxing Moon may take longer to heal.
- **START A NEW RELATIONSHIP/DATING:** With all the upbeat energy, people are more attractive, attentive, and receptive to others.
- **FISHING:** Fish are said to be most active *on* the full and new Moons but bite best *between* the new and full Moons.
- **NAIL (AND HOOF) TRIMMING:** Folklore tells us to cut our nails (and trim our horses' hooves) in the first two weeks after the new Moon to promote healthy and strong regrowth.
- **WEANING BABIES, COMPANION ANIMALS, AND LIVESTOCK:** Lithuanians taught mothers to wean boys during a waxing Moon and girls during a waning Moon, no doubt to make the boys sturdy and the girls slim and delicate.

- **ENTERTAIN/HOST A PARTY:** The positive energy during this phase encourages people to be relaxed and in good spirits.
- **MARRIAGE:** Most believe that getting married and setting up a home together during a growing Moon ensures that the relationship will be a happy and prosperous one. Greeks think marriages consummated during the full Moon are most likely to flourish and succeed. All agree the waning Moon bodes ill for wedded bliss and should be avoided because of dark and negative emotions, anger, and arguments.

Full Moon

As a magical and powerful time of culmination and positive results, this is an ideal phase to make positive changes and tackle challenging issues in your life. You have a much better chance of realizing a desired outcome if you take action during a full Moon.

- **CELEBRATIONS:** Some say festivities are best and most well attended on the full Moon or as close to the full Moon as possible. An event held during a dark Moon at the end of the lunar cycle will attract only a few people. Others say to avoid holding any get-togethers during the run-up to a full Moon because this has been shown to be the time when people are most emotional and conflicts can erupt more easily.
- **MARRIAGE PROPOSALS:** The full Moon is believed to be an ideal time to accept a proposal of marriage.
- **CRABBING, SHRIMPING, AND CLAMMING:** These activities are best when the Moon is full, as all these creatures are active and on the move for mating purposes, making them easy to catch.
- **SIGNING A CONTRACT:** The first three days of the full Moon are the perfect time to sign a contract if you want to experience fairness and honesty throughout the term of the agreement. Whether you are exchanging contracts on a house, applying for a bank loan, or signing a contract of employment, the power of the full Moon will guarantee that the exchange will go through smoothly without any hitches.

- **HUMAN, LIVESTOCK, AND COMPANION ANIMAL CONCEPTION:** Creatures of the sea all follow the phases of the Moon when they are breeding, ensuring that they mate successfully when the pull of the Moon is at its greatest. This is thought to be true for humans and tertiary animals as well.

Waning Phase

About three to ten days after the full Moon, we experience the energy of the waning Moon. This is the ideal time for harvesting, retarding growth, and banishing unwanted habits and things from our lives. The waning Moon is helpful in expelling unhealthy relationships or attitudes from your life.

- **MOWING GRASS, CHOPPING TIMBER, AND CUTTING WOOD:** To slow regrowth of your lawn, cut it during the waning Moon. Although it is said Swedes would not fell a tree in the waning phase of the Moon because it was believed that the wood would shrink and decay.
- **DECELERATE HAIR GROWTH:** If you want your hair to grow as slowly as possible, you should cut, shave, and remove hair during the waning phase of the Moon.
- **SURGERY TO REMOVE:** As a time of harvest and banishing, this is the time for surgery to eradicate something from your body, such as a skin cancer or tumor.
- **HAIR COLORING/DYEING:** If you want your hair color to last longer and be in the best condition, then making changes during the waning phase of the Moon is ideal. This is when changes to the hair, such as hair coloring, will do the least damage and have the best success.
- **END A RELATIONSHIP/QUIT A JOB:** If you want something gone from your life, now is the time! The waning Moon helps ensure a clean break and facilitates moving on as the new Moon cycles around again.
- **BREAK A HABIT/ADDICTION, SUCH AS SMOKING OR DRINKING:** The waning Moon has been shown to be the best time to quit a bad habit.

- **WEIGHT LOSS:** The best time to lose weight is during a waning Moon. You'll feel the pounds drop off as the Moon gets smaller. Keep telling yourself, "smaller Moon, smaller waistline."

Involve Your Kids!

While you're teaching yourself to take the Moon into consideration, start teaching your children about the Moon's potential effects on their world as well. When should your toddler have a playdate with new friends? When's the best time for your teenager to arrange a job interview? How about signing up for a driving test? When should they try to communicate with a friend who's been giving them a hard time? The same rules apply here as to other meditations. If your child is looking to bring something into more abundance, they should work with a waxing Moon. To decrease the power of an element in their life, they should look to the waning Moon phase. Help your kids check the lunar calendar to use a specific energy to their benefit!

• • •

Although re-engineering your schedule a bit to accommodate some lunar living can take some getting used to, once you adapt your thinking in this manner it becomes second nature. And the rewards can far outweigh the minor effort it requires in the long run! Think about this—you are already wary about scheduling lots of things in your life: you wait for payday to book that vacation, or you think about your work schedule when you plan a night out with friends. Considering the phase of the Moon is another step in ensuring you're doing everything you can to achieve an optimal outcome.

part 4

advanced moon magic

This last part of this book is entitled "Advanced Moon Magic," but it's not out of reach, even for a beginner. It is merely one step up the lunar ladder, so to speak. You can delve into astrology to find out how the Moon impacts your astrological sign, whether you follow a Western, Eastern, or Chinese system. You'll learn how to enhance your Moon magic with a Moon altar that can project you into a higher level of consciousness, and also read about herbal lunar gardening—something that can not only ground you but also help you grow your spirit at the same time. Plus, you'll find recipes for herbal teas and lunar cocktails that can add a bit of merriment to your Moon magic. (And with herbal teas that have no alcohol, the Moon's the limit for imbibing!) Get ready to do some hands-on learning and exploring in this section—using the Moon as your guide!

CHAPTER 17
FOLLOW THE SIGNS: ASTROLOGY

Sun Signs vs. Moon Signs

Just about all of us know our Sun sign (signs such as Aries, Gemini, Pisces, etc.) according to Western astrology, even if we are not true believers in this mystical system. And no wonder we know so much about it—we find daily horoscopes online, and people carry tote bags and wear T-shirts boasting their sign.

You may or may not know that you *also* have an astrological Moon sign, or lunar sign. It never seems to get the spotlight in astrology, but your Moon sign is very important. In fact, for those of you who think that your horoscope is always wrong or consistently have trouble finding romantic partners by Sun sign, you might try looking to your Moon sign, as it might have a larger (but quieter) influence over your life.

First, let's simply define the difference between the two:

- At the time of your birth, the position of the Sun is your Sun sign (or star sign).
- The position of the Moon at your time of birth is your Moon sign (or lunar sign).

Women and Moon Signs

If you are a female, your Moon sign is especially important, as the Moon has specific female qualities, such as being synched to a woman's menstruation cycle (a complete lunar phase takes approximately 29.5 days and a menstruation cycle is approximately 28 days). Some ancient traditional cultures even saw the Moon as a basis of life, just as women are the ones who give birth. For example, the Incas referred to the Moon as Mama Quilla (sometimes written as Mama Kilya), meaning mother Moon.

Western Astrology: Sun Signs

Western astrology uses symbolism of planets to express our nature and character. These interpretations shown here only represent the surface of Western astrology. This is a complex subject. To become a professional astrologer and a true expert, it takes years of study to fully understand the system.

There are twelve signs in the zodiac and a specific planet rules each. The different Sun signs of the Western zodiac depict personality traits you may have. Discover your sign by finding the month and date you were born and looking up the characteristics of your sign. (The dates given may vary depending upon the source.) Also, four elements (water, fire, earth, air) are associated with each sign and represent another aspect of the personality.

Aries: The Ram

- **DATES:** March 21 to April 20
- **RULED BY:** Mars
- **ELEMENT:** Fire
- **CHARACTER TRAITS:** Aries people have excellent executive abilities. They are spontaneous and generous. People within this fiery sign should guard against becoming too stubborn and must learn to control their emotional behavior. This is a creative sign, born to lead, not to follow...and they are good leaders.

Taurus: The Bull

- **DATES:** April 21 to May 20
- **RULED BY:** Venus
- **ELEMENT:** Earth
- **CHARACTER TRAITS:** Tauruses exhibit self-control and are consistent in what they do. They are true to their partners and make good parents. Hardworking and rarely ill, they are uncomplicated people and easy to get along with. They are warm, grounded, and believe in "making love, not war."

Gemini: The Twins

- **DATES:** May 21 to June 20
- **RULED BY:** Mercury
- **ELEMENT:** Air
- **CHARACTER TRAITS:** Geminis are charming and brilliant, passionate, and detached. The Gemini is definitely a duality and loves change. Communicating with others is their forte and they will consider both sides of any dispute before making a judgment. They catch on quickly and have inquisitive minds.

Cancer: The Crab

- **DATES:** June 21 to July 20
- **RULED BY:** the Moon
- **ELEMENT:** Water
- **CHARACTER TRAITS:** Cancers are sensitive and kind. They are intuitive and loving, but can be prone to worrying too much about the people they care about. Here, we also find a duality, as a Cancer can be up on stage one minute, getting attention from audiences, or living alone on a mountaintop the next.

Leo: The Lion

- **DATES:** July 21 to August 20
- **RULED BY:** the Sun
- **ELEMENT:** Fire
- **CHARACTER TRAITS:** Leos are born to be leaders. They are at ease in powerful positions and love to be there. They can be very generous, but forgive and forget easily. Sometimes they must learn to be a bit more humble. They will give but rarely take.

Virgo: The Virgin

- **DATES:** August 21 to September 20
- **RULED BY:** Mercury
- **ELEMENT:** Earth
- **CHARACTER TRAITS:** Virgos are intelligent and have a great respect for higher education. They are not as emotional as other signs and may judge themselves and others too harshly. Virgos understand the art of conversation and do not complain about hard work. They can be pure of thought and perfectionists, but when their guard is down, they can have a childlike quality.

Libra: The Balance or Scales

- **DATES:** September 21 to October 20
- **RULED BY:** Venus
- **ELEMENT:** Air
- **CHARACTER TRAITS:** Libras are delightful companions. They take great joy in beauty and delight in group efforts. It is important they keep their scales balanced emotionally. They shine in social situations, and when they find the right partner, they are unwavering in their affections.

Scorpio: The Scorpion

- **DATES:** October 21 to November 20
- **RULED BY:** Mars
- **ELEMENT:** Water
- **CHARACTER TRAITS:** A powerful force drives Scorpios. They can have great passion for people or situations, but when it comes to romantic love, temptations can occur if they do not think logically. This sign is intense, magnetic, and fascinating.

Sagittarius: The Archer

- **DATES:** November 21 to December 20
- **RULED BY:** Jupiter
- **ELEMENT:** Fire
- **CHARACTER TRAITS:** People born under the Sagittarius sign are philosophical and make exceptional marriage and business partners. They are adventurous and have a positive nature, offering quality advice to assist anyone. These kind souls are energetic and have a quick wit.

Capricorn: The Goat

- **DATES:** December 21 to January 20
- **RULED BY:** Saturn
- **ELEMENT:** Earth
- **CHARACTER TRAITS:** Capricorns are the hardest-working sign of the zodiac. They are very independent. They are achievers in the highest sense, demonstrating great depth and sincerity. They are physically alluring, but cautious when it comes to romantic issues. To be a Capricorn is to be successful, because they make it happen through pure ambition.

Aquarius: The Water Bearer

- **DATES:** January 21 to February 20
- **RULED BY:** Uranus
- **ELEMENT:** Air
- **CHARACTER TRAITS:** Aquarius people are gifted in many areas and often achieve fame. They do best when they listen to their own feelings and do not take the advice of others. A sign of intuition, they are seers. They are not loud or demanding. They are modest and unselfish, yet sometimes can appear aloof.

Pisces: The Fishes

- **DATES:** February 21 to March 20
- **RULED BY:** Jupiter and Neptune
- **ELEMENT:** Water
- **CHARACTER TRAITS:** Pisces people are social butterflies. Emotional, sentimental, and romantic qualities make this sign popular. They tend to have a difficult time making decisions—to the point of feeling a bit sorry for themselves. A Pisces has the ability to shine light into dark corners and can be a supportive friend.

Element Meanings in Western Astrology

- **FIRE (ARIES, LEO, AND SAGITTARIUS):** The fire signs are happy and energetic people.
- **EARTH (TAURUS, VIRGO, AND CAPRICORN):** The earth signs are "down to earth," have common sense, and are practical.
- **AIR (GEMINI, LIBRA, AND AQUARIUS):** The air signs are those that contemplate ideas and situations deeply.
- **WATER (CANCER, SCORPIO, AND PISCES):** The water signs are emotional, perceptive, and sensitive.

I recommend seeking further information if you want in-depth analysis of Western astrology.

Eastern Astrology: Under the Moon's Influence

Determining your Moon sign is as easy as finding a website and plugging in some basic information, such as the date, time, and place of your birth. If you know the exact minute you were born, this information will yield the most accurate information regarding your Moon sign. The Hay House Moon Sign Calculator (http://moon-sign-calculator.com/) is a good one to try. If using this site, make sure you put it in the correct time zone. Astrology Library also has a good source: https://astrolibrary.org/moon-sign-calculator.

The Moon sign calculator will tell you what position the Moon was in at the time you were born, which is to say which lunar influences were at play when you entered this world. The reason it's so important to know the exact time of your birth is because while Sun signs each have about a month to work a particular segment of cosmic energy, Moon signs change fairly quickly, with each lasting about 2.5 days!

According to Eastern astrologers, your Moon sign has less to do with your outward personality traits (the things others notice about you) and more to do with what makes you feel safe, good, and "at home," and is therefore tied to the quieter, more instinctual parts of your being. These might be the things you do without even thinking.

Let's say that your Sun sign is Capricorn and your Moon sign is Pisces. People may see that as a Capricorn, you're a real go-getter, above the fray and emotional tangles of the workplace. But the reality of the Pisces Moon sign is that you love feeling—happy, sad, love, whatever the emotion. Sometimes when a Sun sign doesn't seem to "fit" a person, it's because that person's Moon sign pulls him or her in another direction.

Moon sign traits may include:

- **ARIES:** Charisma and accomplishment combine with modesty to make Moon in Aries downplay achievements.

- **TAURUS:** You know you're always right. You have a gut instinct that you need to follow and can't rest if you feel you're going against it.
- **GEMINI:** You're a great communicator and can read what others are thinking before they say it.
- **CANCER:** You love to help others. It makes you feel at peace in your life and in the world.
- **LEO:** The Leo lunar influence may lead to impulsivity at times, which feels right to you… But try slowing down to take in more information before jumping into action.
- **VIRGO:** Moon sign in Virgo can result in feeling that you're immersed in everything around you, which can lead to feeling overwhelmed. Take time to decompress.
- **LIBRA:** You may yearn for a minimalism in every area in your work and personal relationships. Moon in Libra strives to find the simplicity in life.
- **SCORPIO:** Privacy is not a luxury for Moon in Scorpio; it's a visceral need. Take the time to remove yourself from social and work-related chaos every now and then.
- **SAGITTARIUS:** You are philosophical and form great lifelong partnerships. Your nature is positive and you like adventure.
- **CAPRICORN:** You thrive on organization, goal setting, and accomplishment. Without these mileposts, you feel adrift in the world.
- **AQUARIUS:** Perseverance. You have the need to follow things through to the end and may not be able to rest until a project is complete.
- **PISCES:** Emotions are at play with a Moon sign in Pisces. Let emotions move through you and embrace them.

I've been asked what happens if someone is born with the same Sun and Moon sign (for example, someone born on July 7 under a Cancer Moon). This combination simply underscores the Cancer personality traits that are already present. A person with this particular Sun and Moon sign would be compassionate to a fault, perhaps, and would need to make sure to draw limits for giving away his or her energy to others.

Chinese Astrology

Chinese astrology assigns personality traits to those who are born in specific phases of the Moon:

- **FULL MOON:** Careful with words and actions; very diplomatic
- **NEW MOON:** Seeks new experiences and adventures
- **WAXING MOON:** Diligent and loyal
- **WANING MOON:** Mellow and calm

However, for the most part, Chinese astrology is based on twelve animals representing a twelve-year cycle based on the lunar calendar. They use these zodiac animals as a system to characterize a person's personality and their very nature according to the year in which they were born.

To discover what animal sign represents you, see the following list. Simply find your year of birth and the corresponding animal. The characteristics of these animals are said to represent some of your main personality traits.

Meanings of the Elements in Chinese Astrology

You will also see an element listed with each year: metal, wood, water, or earth. By adding in the the elements, you can see differences between two people of the same animal sign but born in different years. Example: someone born in 1990 is a Horse and their element is Metal, making him or her a Metal Horse. While someone born in the year 2002 is also a Horse, his or her element sign is Water. These two people have commonalties, yet there are still subtle differences.

Following is more about each element.

Metal

- Positive aspects of your personality: Determination, flare for speaking, being self-assured, powerful and energized disposition. A self-made person.
- Aspects that need some transformation: Stubborn attitude, not always being reasonable and using common sense.
- Message from your path of evolution: "Lighten up and think about what others have to say. You will not lose strength but only gain respect from others for listening to both sides."

Wood

- Positive aspects of your personality: Being creative and artistic, a moral individual, unselfish and compassionate, adventuresome and always willing to learn.
- Aspects that need some transformation: Too idealistic, passive.
- Message from your path of evolution: "Finish what you start. Stay constant and do not jump from one project to the other unless they can all be accomplished successfully."

Water

- Positive aspects of your personality: Total sensitivity to its highest degree. You are a thinker and a diplomat, persuasive in a gentle yet firm way. You "get it" as far as understanding how people think and what their needs are.
- Aspects that need some transformation: Overly patient. Don't wait too long before you let your voice be heard.
- Message from your path of evolution: "Don't let emotions cloud your common sense. Do what is best for you and it will most likely be what is best for everyone involved. Be a little selfish and it will work with you, not against you."

Fire

- Positive aspects of your personality: Leadership, "movers and shakers," passionate and aggressive, totally confident, excellent communication skills.
- Aspects that need some transformation: Sometimes self-serving, impatient, and not understanding of others' points of view, as well as a possible workaholic.
- Message from your path of evolution: "Be composed. Stop and smell the roses. Use your fiery passion for love...not just business."

Earth

- Positive aspects of your personality: Wisdom, stability, logical nature, and reliability. Industrious and serious money-making abilities. Unspoken sexuality in the most primitive sense.
- Aspects that need some transformation: Lack of imagination at times, a creative nature that is hidden because you feel you have not earned the right to relax yet in life.
- Message from your path of evolution: "Get a little wild! Do something that is not like you and is not predictable. Tell people you care about how you really feel."

In the Chinese tradition, everything has a yin and a yang—which is to say that everything has a positive/passive/female and a negative/active/male "aspect." But everything also changes. Confused yet? Here's an example. Let's say you were born on February 1, 1990. You are a Horse born under an "active" (+) sign; however, the following year, your sign reversed and went into "passive" (–) mode. To know where your sign is now, you can simply do some math (every tenth year would be passive if you are born under an active sign, and vice versa), or you can google to see which element your sign is in this year.

YEAR	FROM – TO	ANIMAL	ELEMENT	ASPECT
1930	30 January 1930 – 16 February 1931	Horse	Metal	+
1931	17 February 1931 – 5 February 1932	Sheep	Metal	–
1932	6 February 1932 – 25 January 1933	Monkey	Water	+
1933	26 January 1933 – 13 February 1934	Rooster	Water	–
1934	14 February 1934 – 3 February 1935	Dog	Wood	+
1935	4 February 1935 – 23 January 1936	Pig	Wood	–
1936	24 January 1936 – 10 February 1937	Rat	Fire	+
1937	11 February 1937 – 30 January 1938	Ox	Fire	–
1938	31 January 1938 – 18 February 1939	Tiger	Earth	+
1939	19 February 1939 – 7 February 1940	Rabbit	Earth	–
1940	8 February 1940 – 26 January 1941	Dragon	Metal	+
1941	27 January 1941 – 14 February 1942	Snake	Metal	–
1942	15 February 1942 – 4 February 1943	Horse	Water	+
1943	5 February 1943 – 24 January 1944	Sheep	Water	–
1944	25 January 1944 – 12 February 1945	Monkey	Wood	+
1945	13 February 1945 – 1 February 1946	Rooster	Wood	–
1946	2 February 1946 – 21 January 1947	Dog	Fire	+
1947	22 January 1947 – 9 February 1948	Pig	Fire	–
1948	10 February 1948 – 28 January 1949	Rat	Earth	+
1949	29 January 1949 – 16 February 1950	Ox	Earth	–
1950	17 February 1950 – 5 February 1951	Tiger	Metal	+
1951	6 February 1951 – 26 January 1952	Rabbit	Metal	–
1952	27 January 1952 – 13 February 1953	Dragon	Water	+

YEAR	FROM – TO	ANIMAL	ELEMENT	ASPECT
1953	14 February 1953 – 2 February 1954	Snake	Water	–
1954	3 February 1954 – 23 January 1955	Horse	Wood	+
1955	24 January 1955 – 11 February 1956	Sheep	Wood	–
1956	12 February 1956 – 30 January 1957	Monkey	Fire	+
1957	31 January 1957 – 17 February 1958	Rooster	Fire	–
1958	18 February 1958 – 7 February 1959	Dog	Earth	+
1959	8 February 1959 – 27 January 1960	Pig	Earth	–
1960	28 January 1960 – 14 February 1961	Rat	Metal	+
1961	15 February 1961 – 4 February 1962	Ox	Metal	–
1962	5 February 1962 – 24 January 1963	Tiger	Water	+
1963	25 January 1963 – 12 February 1964	Rabbit	Water	–
1964	13 February 1964 – 1 February 1965	Dragon	Wood	+
1965	2 February 1965 – 20 January 1966	Snake	Wood	–
1966	21 January 1966 – 8 February 1967	Horse	Fire	+
1967	9 February 1967 – 29 January 1968	Sheep	Fire	–
1968	30 January 1968 – 16 February 1969	Monkey	Earth	+
1969	17 February 1969 – 5 February 1970	Rooster	Earth	–
1970	6 February 1970 – 26 January 1971	Dog	Metal	+
1971	27 January 1971 – 15 January 1972	Pig	Metal	–
1972	16 January 1972 – 2 February 1973	Rat	Water	+
1973	3 February 1973 – 22 January 1974	Ox	Water	–
1974	23 January 1974 – 10 February 1975	Tiger	Wood	+
1975	11 February 1975 – 30 January 1976	Rabbit	Wood	–

YEAR	FROM – TO	ANIMAL	ELEMENT	ASPECT
1976	31 January 1976 – 17 February 1977	Dragon	Fire	+
1977	18 February 1977 – 6 February 1978	Snake	Fire	–
1978	7 February 1978 – 27 January 1979	Horse	Earth	+
1979	28 January 1979 – 15 February 1980	Sheep	Earth	–
1980	16 February 1980 – 4 February 1981	Monkey	Metal	+
1981	5 February 1981 – 24 January 1982	Rooster	Metal	–
1982	25 January 1982 – 12 February 1983	Dog	Water	+
1983	13 February 1983 – 1 February 1984	Pig	Water	–
1984	2 February 1984 – 19 February 1985	Rat	Wood	+
1985	20 February 1985 – 8 February 1986	Ox	Wood	–
1986	9 February 1986 – 28 January 1987	Tiger	Fire	+
1987	29 January 1987 – 16 February 1988	Rabbit	Fire	–
1988	17 February 1988 – 5 February 1989	Dragon	Earth	+
1989	6 February 1989 – 26 January 1990	Snake	Earth	–
1990	27 January 1990 – 14 February 1991	Horse	Metal	+
1991	15 February 1991 – 3 February 1992	Sheep	Metal	–
1992	4 February 1992 – 22 January 1993	Monkey	Water	+
1993	23 January 1993 – 9 February 1994	Rooster	Water	–
1994	10 February 1994 – 30 January 1995	Dog	Wood	+
1995	31 January 1995 – 18 February 1996	Pig	Wood	–
1996	19 February 1996 – 7 February 1997	Rat	Fire	+
1997	8 February 1997 – 27 January 1998	Ox	Fire	–
1998	28 January 1998 – 15 February 1999	Tiger	Earth	+

YEAR	FROM – TO	ANIMAL	ELEMENT	ASPECT
1999	16 February 1999 – 4 February 2000	Rabbit	Earth	–
2000	5 February 2000 – 23 January 2001	Dragon	Metal	+
2001	24 January 2001 – 11 February 2002	Snake	Metal	–
2002	12 February 2002 – 31 January 2003	Horse	Water	+
2003	1 February 2003 – 21 January 2004	Sheep	Water	–
2004	22 January 2004 – 8 February 2005	Monkey	Wood	+
2005	9 February 2005 – 28 January 2006	Rooster	Wood	–
2006	29 January 2006 – 17 February 2007	Dog	Fire	+
2007	18 February 2007 – 6 February 2008	Pig	Fire	–
2008	7 February 2008 – 25 January 2009	Rat	Earth	+
2009	26 January 2009 – 13 February 2010	Ox	Earth	–
2010	14 February 2010 – 2 February 2011	Tiger	Metal	+
2011	3 February 2011 – 22 January 2012	Rabbit	Metal	–
2012	23 January 2012 – 9 February 2013	Dragon	Water	+
2013	10 February 2013 – 30 January 2014	Snake	Water	–
2014	31 January 2014 – 18 February 2015	Horse	Wood	+
2015	19 February 2015 – 7 February 2016	Sheep	Wood	–
2016	8 February 2016 – 27 January 2017	Monkey	Fire	+
2017	28 January 2017 – 15 February 2018	Rooster	Fire	–
2018	16 February 2018 – 4 February 2019	Dog	Earth	+
2019	5 February 2019 – 24 January 2020	Pig	Earth	–
2020	25 January 2020 – 11 February 2021	Rat	Metal	+
2021	12 February 2021 – 31 January 2022	Ox	Metal	–

YEAR	FROM – TO	ANIMAL	ELEMENT	ASPECT
2022	1 February 2022 – 21 January 2023	Tiger	Water	+
2023	22 January 2023 – 9 February 2024	Rabbit	Water	–
2024	10 February 2012 – 28 January 2025	Dragon	Wood	+
2025	29 January 2025 – 16 February 2026	Snake	Wood	–
2026	17 February 2026 – 5 February 2027	Horse	Fire	+
2027	6 February 2027 – 25 January 2028	Sheep	Fire	–
2028	26 January 2028 – 12 February 2029	Monkey	Earth	+
2029	13 February 2029 – 2 February 2030	Rooster	Earth	–
2030	3 February 2030 – 22 January 2031	Dog	Metal	+
2031	23 January 2031 – 10 February 2032	Pig	Metal	–
2032	11 February 2032 – 30 January 2033	Rat	Water	+
2033	31 January 2033 – 18 February 2034	Ox	Water	–
2034	19 February 2034 – 7 February 2035	Tiger	Wood	+
2035	8 February 2035 – 27 January 2036	Rabbit	Wood	–
2036	28 January 2036 – 14 February 2037	Dragon	Fire	+
2037	15 February 2037 – 3 February 2038	Snake	Fire	–
2038	4 February 2038 – 23 January 2039	Horse	Earth	+
2039	24 January 2039 – 11 February 2040	Sheep	Earth	–
2040	12 February 2040 – 31 January 2041	Monkey	Metal	+
2041	1 February 2041 – 21 January 2042	Rooster	Metal	–
2042	22 January 2042 – 9 February 2043	Dog	Water	+
2043	10 February 2043 – 29 January 2044	Pig	Water	–

The Characteristics of the Animal Zodiac Signs in Chinese Astrology

The Rat: Charm and Intelligence

Those born under the influence of the Rat are dynamic and usually have active lives. They exhibit extremes when it comes to money matters, being too generous at times and too frugal at other times. Rats are not couch potatoes and love adventure and thrill seeking. They have great control over their romantic feelings yet are highly sensual once you get to know them.

The Ox: Enterprise and Stability

Those born under the influence of the Ox have a lot of common sense and are very practical. They are not against hard work and will strive until they reach their goals. They are faithful and fall in love slowly, expecting their partners to do the same.

The Tiger: Bravery and Protection

Those born under the influence of the Tiger tend to attract people and are always ready to fight for a just cause. They create their own reality and like to do things their way. They can tend to be flirtations and filled with eroticism.

The Rabbit: Humbleness and Family Life

Those born under the influence of the Rabbit are extremely good-natured. Because of their sensitive nature, you will find many Rabbits in the creative fields. Rabbits do not like to argue and will tend to mate with easygoing people.

The Dragon: Luck and Good Fortune

Those born under the influence of the Dragon can fit in with almost any type of crowd or situation. The opposite sex is extremely drawn to the Dragon. While the Dragon has strong physical attractions, an individual's intelligence can be just as stimulating to them, as well.

The Snake: Wisdom and Wit

Those born under the influence of the Snake are mystical and mysterious. They are excellent with money matters and seemed to live charmed lives. They are mostly above-average in physical appearance and look for a mate that is above-average in all areas. Success and power are turnons for most Snakes.

The Horse: Refinement and Eagerness

Those born under the influence of the Horse tend to have many friends and a sense of humor, as well as being enthusiastic and learning quickly. When you meet a Horse for the first time, you may feel as if you have known him or her for years. Love can make the normally practical Horse be disposed to not thinking clearly. They also tend to fall in love too easily yet often settle down later in life.

The Goat (or Sheep): The Arts and Sensitivity

Those born under the influence of the Goat are peaceful people. They do not want to cause undue problems or chaos. They are mostly team players and would rather be part of a group than working on their own. Goats love their home and would rather be married or in a partnership than single. Goats by nature are affectionate and love to be loved.

The Monkey: Imagination and Popularity

Those born under the influence of the Monkey are inventive and can come to correct conclusions about people, places, and things immediately. The Monkey has a tendency to get bored quickly, which causes them to change romantic partners often. However, once they decide to finally settle down, they make intriguing and exciting partners.

The Rooster: Flamboyance and Confidence

Those born under the influence of the Rooster are very organized and have control over their business affairs. They love attention and enjoy entertaining. Roosters will be faithful once they find someone with whom they are truly happy. However, this could take them some time as they can alienate a potentially good partner with their sometimes critical remarks. Because they pride themselves on their honesty, they are usually monogamous in relationships and never "kiss and tell."

The Dog: Loyalty and Protection

Those born under the influence of the Dog are great humanitarians. They will lend a hand to a friend or stranger in times of need and look for nothing in return. This sign is not materialistic, and they put a loving partner above all things. Once they find their romantic match they will stay with their partner though sunshine and storms.

The Pig: Honesty and Harmony

Those born under the influence of the Pig love to be surrounded by beautiful things. They love to live in the height of luxury and feel they are well worth it. They don't mind working hard and getting their hands dirty, but in return they will indulge themselves in a reward. The entertaining they do is "all or nothing." They roll out the red carpet for their friends. Pigs do not allow their sexual desires go unattended. They immensely enjoy the gratification of their intimate partner and are devoted to the ones they love.

Chinese Zodiac Compatibility Chart

This chart will show you the animal symbols of the zodiac with whom you are most likely to get along well. Find your animal symbol and check underneath for your compatibles.

- **RAT:** Compatible with other Rats, Ox, Dragon, Monkey, Tiger, Snake, Rooster, Dog, and Pig.
- **OX:** Compatible with the Rat, Rabbit, Snake, Rooster, Monkey, Dog, Pig, and Ox.

- **TIGER:** Compatible with the Pig, Dog, Horse, Goat, Rat, Rabbit, and Rooster.
- **RABBIT:** Compatible with the Goat, Snake, Pig, Ox, Tiger, Dragon, Horse, Monkey, and Rabbit.
- **DRAGON:** Compatible with the Snake, Rat, Monkey, Rooster, Rabbit, Pig, Horse, Goat, and Dragon.
- **SNAKE:** Compatible with the Ox, Rabbit, Rooster, Rat, Horse, Goat, Monkey, and Dog.
- **HORSE:** Compatible with the Tiger, Goat, Rooster, Dog, Rabbit, Dragon, Snake, Pig, and Horse.
- **GOAT:** Compatible with the Tiger, Horse, Monkey, Pig, Rabbit, Dragon, Snake, Rooster, and Goat.
- **MONKEY:** Compatible with the Rat, Dragon, Pig, Monkey, Goat, Ox, Rabbit, Snake, and Dog.
- **DOG:** Compatible with the Horse, Pig, Tiger, Monkey, Rat, Ox, Rabbit, Snake, and Dog.
- **PIG:** Compatible with the Goat, Rabbit, Dog, Tiger, Pig, Dragon, Ox, Horse, and Rat.

Here are some websites that contain more information for those who want to investigate further regarding Chinese zodiac signs; visit https://en.wikipedia.org/wiki/Chinese_zodiac or https://chinese-zodiac-signs.com/.

• • •

I know people who combine astrology traditions—for example, they follow the Chinese zodiac, but they swear that their Moon sign plays a large part in making them who they are. And why not? The heavens are big enough for all of these ideas and traditions!

CHAPTER 18

CREATING A MOON ALTAR

What's Different about a Moon Altar?

For those of you who would like to take your Moon magic to another level, you can create a Moon altar. A "regular" altar is, in essence, a dedicated space where you put spiritual or religious objects used for meditation, prayer, divination, visualization, or anything that will enhance these practices. These traditions are always connected to your higher power, whether that is God, nature, gods and goddesses, and so forth. An altar can display anything that is sacred to you, such as statues, gemstones, candles, and pictures. Anything goes, as long as it is of a positive nature and harms no one.

When you add a Moon symbol of some type to your altar, you are not worshipping the Moon but rather using the Moon's energy for that extra lunar boost to project your thoughts, desires, meditations, and prayers out into the universe. This way, your request is enhanced or magnified. If you are not asking for anything except messages or guidance for what it is you desire, they tend to come in clearer with a Moon symbol incorporated in your altar as you are enhancing your heightened state of consciousness, remembering the intensity of the Moon phase. I always feel that a place devoted to a divine energy is a portal or threshold that takes you to a place where you can communicate more easily with the spiritual being of your understanding.

Creating Your Altar

Your altar is completely customizable—it can be as small or as large, as simple or as ornate, and as filled or as sparse as you like. The following are some guidelines to consider as you plan your altar.

Location

When you are deciding where to locate your altar, use common sense first and foremost. You can make one inside or outside, but if you live in an apartment, you are most likely going to have an inside altar unless you have a balcony or outside space that you can utilize. If you have acres of land and decide to put your altar somewhere in the north forty, keep your safety in mind. Communing with positive energy is difficult if there are animals on the prowl! If you are in the suburbs and have a small yard and decide to construct a huge altar outside for all of your neighbors to see, this could have its drawbacks too—namely, being distracted by your neighbors watching you or blaring their music.

Also, be mindful of others if you live in close quarters. Chanting in the middle of the night and playing your drum to reach an altered state of consciousness when there is two feet between you and your roommate is just too much. Always bear in mind that an altar site should be a place without chaos that you can retreat to for serenity.

Altar Platform or Base

You can use almost any platform as an altar base. It can be a large or small table, pedestal, bedroom dresser, or part of anything solid. The important thing is that is that the altar is not wobbly, especially if you have breakable items on it and if you will be adding candles. Improvise! Here are some ideas to think about:

- Stack storage bins and use the top as a platform.
- Have a sturdy, dry windowsill? That will do nicely; just don't light candles near any drapes.

- Use an empty shelf of a bookcase.
- Are you really a private person? Consider a shelf in a linen closet that provides ample space and can be closed up when you're finished.
- Cement blocks work well, especially outside. For other outside spaces, think about tree stumps and such.
- Look to the thrift stores and garage sales for suitable surfaces too.

Your altar will become your go-to place when you are in need of comfort or a spiritual boost. It is a place where you will spend alone time with your higher power, so you want it to be a place that gives you a feeling of tranquility.

Having discussed all sorts of altar surfaces, here's one caveat: don't use something that is associated with negativity. Let's say you have an old table that you and your ex battled for in your divorce. It will probably not be the best place for you to place your scared items in an effort to connect with your universal life force. Even if you are using cardboard boxes with your old clothes in them, that's better than something you associate with pessimism. It's also important that the altar and everything placed on it is clean. Clean keeps chaos and its associated energy away.

What to Place on Your Altar

Just as your altar construction is as unique as you, so too will be the items you put on the altar.

Sample Moon altar.

Cloth

You may want to cover your altar with a cloth of some type. This can be any kind of fabric that you like—a remnant from a fabric store, a pillowcase, or a cool placemat you like. Again, make sure it's washed and clean. The idea of covering your altar base is to make it look appealing. It also separates the base from your spiritual tools and makes them more special and more protected.

Moon Phase Images

Since this is a Moon altar, you will need a depiction of the Moon on it. You can use one Moon phase picture, or you can have pictures of all the different phases and change them according to the current phase. You might even want to frame them. You can draw an image yourself as well.

Even if you aren't an artist, it's simple to draw any of the lunar images.

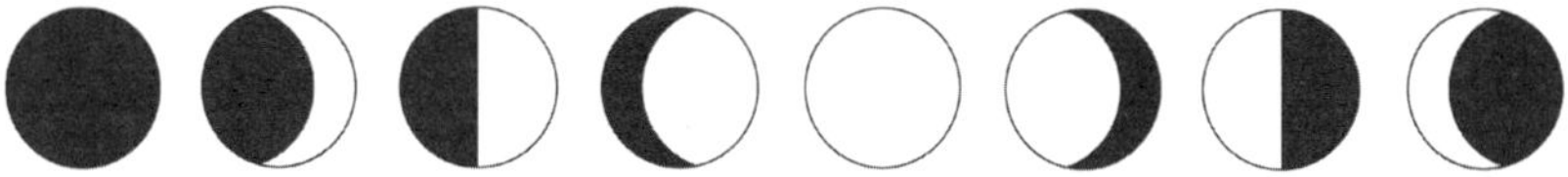

Moon phases, from left to right: new Moon, waxing crescent Moon, first quarter Moon, waxing gibbous Moon, full Moon, waning gibbous Moon, last quarter Moon, waning crescent Moon.

A Representation of Your Higher Power

Next, add something that represents the divine or your higher power. This should be placed in the center of your altar. It might be a cross or a statue of Jesus or Buddha; it might even be a god or goddess statue. If you believe in universal life force energy, you might use a large crystal. (See "Adding Crystals and Gemstones to Your Altar" in this chapter for more information.)

Candles

Candles can correspond to the three levels in life in which we exist (body, mind, and spirit):

- The wax or base of the candle represents our physical body.
- The wick represents our minds.
- The flame represents our spirit and the divine.

So to have a candle on any altar is a reminder of the divine's presence in your ritual, meditation, or prayer.

Carving or Writing on Candles

You can also carve the current phase of the Moon on your candle for your meditation. Even a pen or marker on the candle will work for drawing a Moon phase symbol. If you want to put other keywords that pertain to your meditation on the candle, you can. Once you have the phase of the Moon printed or carved (toothpicks work well for carving), you can add a few things to the candle as well. For example: the words "new computer," or draw what looks like a computer to you. You can write "love" or make a heart. How about dollar signs for that pay increase? The more fun you have with these meditations, the more you relax. The more you relax, the more confidence you have. The more confidence you have, the more you can expand your thoughts to manifest your future.

Candle Colors and Their Meanings

Different color candles draw on different energy, so have fun with this!

- **WHITE:** When in doubt, always use white. It is powerful and pure and also enhances work or meditations regarding psychic skills or divination, healing, and peace.
- **BLACK:** Removes negative energy. Release, discharging, banishing, and reversing.
- **BLUE:** Communication, protection, healing, devotion, weight loss, harmony, and loyalty.
- **BROWN:** Stability, lost items, animals, protection, telepathy, success, and wealth.

- **GREEN:** Prosperity, accomplishment, new careers or jobs, love, nature, and diffuses jealousy.
- **LAVENDER (LIGHTER THAN PURPLE):** Spirituality, inspiration, attracts sprit help, and calming of stress.
- **ORANGE:** Emotional healing, self-control, new friends, cleansing of those with attitudes, luck, business deal or opportunities. Also winning, courage, and achievement.
- **PINK:** Romance, affection, love, forming partnerships, all feminine endeavors, respect, pride, devotion, happiness, and unconditional love.
- **PURPLE (DARKER THAN LAVENDER):** Anything pertaining to intuition, psychic abilities, or divination. Ancient wisdom, contacting those on the other side, protection, and meditation.
- **RED:** Sexual passion, fertility, energy, anything fast, willpower, strength, attraction with vigor for what you desire, such as health and charisma.
- **SILVER:** Developing psychic abilities, removing negativity that may surround you, victory, and neutralization of bad situations. It has a calming effect.
- **YELLOW:** Studying, intelligence, logic, pleasantness, memory, endurance, past-life recollection, all things glamorous, desirability and attraction, confidence, and safekeeping.

Other Items to Include

You can include anything on your altar that means something to you and makes you smile. Optional items you might want to consider:

- **A DECORATIVE BELL.** You may want to ring a bell to begin a meditation and invoke divine powers. A bell is also used to clear the field of negativity entering your space. Ring as many times as you feel are needed.
- **DIVINATION TOOLS.** If you are doing any type of divination, you will need tarot cards, pendulums, or a cup of tea to do your tea leaf reading.

- **LIGHTER.** Remember, if you are using candles or incense, you will need matches or a lighter.
- **A CHALICE, CUP, GLASS, OR ANY VESSEL OF YOUR CHOOSING.** Chalices are used typically for wine, juices, or water. A chalice is connected with our feminine side as it represents the element of water, which is associated with the womb, emotions, and desire. Using a chalice during meditation is often thought of as a bridge between thought and action. As you meditate, you may want to take a sip at a time it seems appropriate to think about how you are going to take action for your desire. You can also have a taste to close your meditation or ritual. This is considered an offering to the universe or divine. (Just don't overdo your offering. Notice I used the words *sip* and *taste*. No gulping through your entire meditation or rite.)
- **PEN AND PAPER.** If you want to write your desires down, you will need something with which to write.
- **POT OR ASHTRAY.** Bring an iron pot, large ashtray, or anything that contains fire safely if you plan on burning incense or if you are writing down a desire and sending it up in smoke to the universe.
- **FLOWERS.** Flowers beautify your space and give off a feeling of joy and contentment.

Once you place your main representation of your higher power, add the other items in any spot you like. The important factor is that it feels right to you. Keep moving things around until your intuition says, "Yes, that's it...perfect."

- **OUTSIDE ITEMS:** If you are planning an outside altar, think about which materials are durable enough to withstand the weather, or think about items that are portable enough to tote inside and outside. A concrete statue may work well for a centerpiece. Candles and flowers are simple additions and easy enough to carry outdoors.

Think Twice Before Including Things That Make You Sad

A picture of your dog that has passed may make you cry or feel blue. It's best to leave those kinds of things elsewhere in the house, as this is not a time to be sad.

However, if you are trying to receive messages from a loved one, you may want to put his or her picture on the altar for that session. I would not recommend leaving it there permanently since your altar is for many uses and not meant as a shrine to one individual. (Though you could make a separate area for this purpose.)

Adding Crystals and Gemstones to Your Altar

Crystals and gemstones, like incense and colored candles, correspond to certain situations or help boost specific energies. To many healers and New Age believers, the power of the positive and healing energy that comes from the earth is absorbed into these particular stones. It should be noted that when I refer to gemstones or crystals, they do not have to be polished. They can be in their natural state. You can purchase gemstones online, in New Age gift stores, and in gem shops. Sometimes souvenir stores sell them, especially in places that are known for their regional gems. There is no need to spend a lot of money on any gemstone unless you can afford it or you really want to. A few dollars goes a long way when it comes to giving your altar a little oomph.

Any gemstones suggested for healing should not be used as a substitute for regular medical treatment. These are only suggestions you might want to consider along with what your medical professional or healer suggests. Always seek professional help when dealing with health-related problems.

When buying a crystal, pick it up, touch it, feel it. How does it feel to you? If you like the sensation you experience, it has found its home with you. I think crystals find and pick you. However, if the one that picks you happens to be the five-hundred-dollar type, keep looking unless you can afford it. There is more than one crystal that will do the job.

The following are a few of the basic qualities of the most familiar stones and crystals for a quick reference.

Clear Quartz Crystal

Clear quartz crystal is the universal go-to crystal for everything. It also enhances the properties of other stones around it. It promotes focus, psychic endeavors, healing, and protection.

If you don't know what to include in your meditations, use quartz. Likewise, if you can only buy one crystal, buy quartz. It enhances the Moon's intensity and can amplify, balance, help us focus, and meditate. Quartz assists you in transmitting your intention. Clear quartz crystals are what give life to your quartz watches, radios, and beloved computers. We would not be living in this age of technology without it!

This broad-spectrum stone will aid you in meditation and healing. Quartz can also negate negative psychic arrows of attack that may come from other people, places, or things. I had a friend who used to wear a clear quartz crystal necklace. One day it fell apart. The chain broke and the crystal popped out of the base. She immediately thought it was due to the fact that the necklace must have been cheap and "you get what you pay for." I pointed out to her that the necklace might have taken a "hit" for her and saved her from an ill-meaning psychic attack. Perhaps someone was wishing her misfortune or loathing and the necklace blocked that energy!

When buying a clear quartz crystal, it does not have to be totally clear. Some have inclusions, bubbles, are a little misty, and colors can vary.

Amethyst

Amethyst brings healing, dismisses anger, balances you, and provides stability. It's a good choice if you are working on sobriety or addictions.

Carnelian

Carnelian is associated with creativity, stimulates drive, and helps clarify your goals if you are not sure about what you want. This stone is also a stone of protection because it absorbs energy and repels it. I know many people who do ghost hunting and wear carnelian as a form of protection against psychic attack. If you do this, always cleanse or clear your stone before and after a ghost investigation or anywhere you think there are dysfunctional earthbound entities.

Lapis Lazuli

Lapis lazuli has a reputation for healing ailments like insomnia, headaches, high blood pressure, eye strain, and gloominess. On the other hand, it also has a reputation for attracting love. No wonder it can help gloominess and ailments go away...it can help you fall in love! This is a very peaceful stone to wear or display.

Moonstone

Moonstone is an incredibly powerful stone. I don't talk about gift-giving in this book, but there is Moon lore that says if you give a lover a necklace or medallion made of moonstone on the night of a full Moon, you will always have a passionate relationship. You can exchange moonstone necklaces too.

If you don't wear jewelry, a little statue or just the gem itself will work. Keep it in a place of distinction in your home.

Moonstone also brings good fortune, enhances your intuition, and bestows upon you attainment, not only in matters of the heart but also in business dealings. It protects you when you are out to sea or on the water. (But that doesn't mean you should neglect to wear a life preserver!) If you have had a disagreement with a romantic partner, it can aid in reuniting you. In meditation it can give you a sense of who you are and where you are going.

If you feel you need to revitalize your moonstone, place it in the light of a waxing Moon to bring back some of its influence, just like recharging a battery. Stay away from full, new, dark, or waning Moons for recharging your moonstone as they can actually deplete it more. Remember, waning Moons release and take away, dark Moons are somewhat neutral, and full Moons have such energy that it can confuse the vibration.

Rose Quartz

Rose quartz is regarded as the love stone—not only in terms of love of others but also love of oneself. It heals emotions, discharges loneliness, and encourages inner peace.

Turquoise

Turquoise is considered one of the oldest stones in the history of man. It is considered the paramount of all healing stones. It is exceptional. Turquoise has been utilized by all cultures. It is indicative of wisdom and nobility. Turquoise was considered sacred and worn as an adornment for defense, luck, and powerful influence by many cultures. To name a few, ancient Egyptians, Native Americans, Chinese, and Persians all recognized the value of this stone. The Aztec and Inca also gave glory to this magical influence.

This mineral purifies, is advantageous for tissue regeneration, and is said to have anti-inflammatory effects. Some consider it a healer of the whole body. Always bear in mind that these are spiritual supports of healing and should not be considered a prescription of sorts that replaces professional healthcare treatments.

Crystals and Moon Phases

As far as which gemstone to use with a particular Moon phase, there are no rules (with the exception of the moonstone, which I mentioned earlier). It depends on what you are trying to achieve. You have to match the vibrations of that gemstone with your intention. For instance, if you are looking for love, think rose quartz. You should have already picked out the phase of the Moon (which would be waxing or full, by the way). That said, you do not pick gemstones according to the phases of the Moon, but rather to enhance your meditation you have already chosen for that lunar phase.

Incense

In years gone by, it was discovered that burning certain natural aromatic resins and gums would cleanse a space and take away smells of mildew, cooking odors like cabbage or garlic, and other musty odors. Generally speaking, both resins and gums are from sap-like plant and tree secretions, with the resins having a fragrance and the gum binding things together. Hence, these resins and gums (or resin-gums) were used as incense to mask unpleasant smells or maybe remove them altogether. However, these resins were expensive, and the average person could not afford them or they were not able to use them regularly.

When an important guest was coming to visit, incense was burned as a way to welcome company. When you came into someone's home and incense was burning, you knew someone special was on the way (maybe it was YOU). Royals and aristocrats burned incense on special public occasions. Churches and places of worship did the same, as it was a way to welcome the divine.

Today, people burn incense on their personal altars as a way to purify their space and welcome their higher power to their dedicated space of meditation and observance.

There is usually no middle ground when it comes to incense. People either love its wide varieties of forms, sizes, and fragrances or they find it objectionable. Some say it makes them sneeze, gives them headaches, or they feel it permeates their clothes—and not in a good way.

Many people who do not like the scent of incense prefer to use potpourri and essential oils.

Scents and Herbs and Their Corresponding Moon Magic Uses

Different fragrances, scents, and herbs can correspond to certain intentions when doing Moon magic.

SPIRITUAL INTENTIONS:
- Carnation
- Frankincense
- Jasmine
- Pine
- Rose
- Sage
- Sandalwood

LOVE:
- Apple
- Basil
- Chamomile
- Jasmine
- Musk
- Peppermint
- Rose

HEALTH:
- Cedar
- Eucalyptus
- Lemon balm
- Myrrh
- Pine
- Sage
- Thyme

CAREER/OCCUPATION:
- Bayberry
- Clove
- Honeysuckle
- Mint
- Sage
- Vanilla
- Wisteria

This is not a comprehensive list. There are many more fragrances that are known to influence brain activity. For example, citrus fragrances promote energy, and the smell of lavender is known to be calming.

Moon Altar Ritual to Send Off Your Thoughts and Desires

Here is a simple way to send your message up and out.

1. Once you are in front of your altar—and in an altered state of consciousness—write down what it is you want in a positive manner. Example: *I desire to have that company call me and tell me they have chosen me for the job in Boston.*

2. Concentrate on what you wrote.
3. When you feel it, it is time to send it off. Light the paper with the candle flame or with a lighter or match and drop it into a fire-safe container. It does not have to burn completely. Just a little is good enough. (Intention, intention, intention!) See your wish going up and out and being released into the cosmos.
4. As always, use a closing thought, such as "Blessed be," "And so it is," "Amen," "Namaste," and so forth.

Altars to Go

An altar doesn't have to be on display all the time. Maybe you would like to have an altar, but for many reasons—such as limited space or having roommates—it's just not reasonable. There is an answer: altars to go. (Being the Capricorn I am, it makes sense to me…it's logical.)

All you need is a container to hold your magical or inspirational tools. Call it your altar box or drawer. You can also keep your items in a bag and grab it when the time comes.

If you decide to do a meditation outside on a particular night, you can open up your altar box and *voila*! It's magic right there with all of your Moon magic needs at your disposal. Going out of town or to a friend's or relative's house? *Ta-da*…there you have it. Camping is great for Moon magic events—hence, the carry-and-go method works like a charm.

Altars in Your Mind

Altars are representative of an encounter with your higher power, the divine, God, gods and goddesses, the universal life source energy, and every other word you can think of to describe that which is a part of the grand picture. But if you're not inclined to gather, place, and take care of all these altar items, here's another suggestion: you can establish an altar in your heart or through visualization. It's simple. Just imagine what you would place on an altar, and once you see it in your mind, you can begin your meditation. You can see the phase of the Moon on the altar, the candle, the bell you might ring, or the incense you might burn.

This is really quite fun and I do it often. With every meditation you can have a new altar in your mind. You can use the best of the best, as money is of no matter when you're visualizing the objects. If you want that candle to have have a diamond and gold pedestal, it's yours! Do you want to burn that expensive, hard-to-find incense? No worries. Even put it in an exquisite incense burner. And please, don't forget to travel to your altar if you want. You can go to an outside altar in England, Ireland, Canada, or India. Feel like leaving the planet? Mars is very nice. You could even do it directly on the Moon if you like!

Getting there is up to you. You can just suddenly see yourself there or you can fly on a sleigh, horse, or magic carpet—be creative. Visualizing your altar time is really interesting and it works! Having your teeth cleaned or a procedure where you are awake but there might be some discomfort? Close your eyes and do a meditation somewhere—any place—but the dentist's office. Take yourself away from the physical now and then and do a Moon meditation with your favorite altar anywhere you like.

• • •

One style of Moon altar is not better than another. However you set up an altar is all up to you, so think about it and make a decision before your Moon magic event to determine what direction you will follow. Try a variety of candles, gems, and other items to see what works for you. Don't underestimate your own power—if you can think it, see it, and feel it, you are three-quarters of the way there.

CHAPTER 19
HERBAL LUNAR GARDENING

Planting/Gardening

What else can you do with your Moon magic? Farmers and gardeners often use the phases of the Moon to plant, and that's where those trusty almanacs, like the *Old Farmer's Almanac,* come in handy. This is a practice begun by our ancestors long ago. How exactly does the Moon affect plants? It all comes down to the gravitational pull on the earth and the presence of water in the soil. Each Moon phase has a different effect on the soil, as you'll read next. It's nature as its best. And of course, nature is magic!

The following list will give you a *very* general idea of planting according to the Moon phases. For detailed suggestions, invest in an almanac or two. Here are some suggestions:

- We all love the *Old Farmer's Almanac* but also look to a few others, such as Greir's online almanac (www.griersalmanac.com), which is a regional almanac for Georgia, Alabama, Louisiana, Arkansas, Oklahoma, Texas, Tennessee, Virginia, Maryland, Florida, North Carolina, South Carolina, Mississippi, Kentucky, and West Virginia. Grier's is a good source of information and can be ordered online. They also offer a free daily update on their site that gives you daily Moon phases, planting tips, astrological events, and more.

- An Irish publication is the *Old Moore's Almanac* (http://oldmooresalmanac.com). Do not confuse this publication with *Old Moore's Almanack* (with a *k*), which is an astrological almanac that was first published in Britain in 1697 and is now published by Foulsham Publishing, putting the focus on the United Kingdom (www.foulsham.com/p/1416/old-moore39s-almanack-2018).
- The website www.chinesefortunecalendar.com/almanac.htm, which is an online Chinese almanac, tells us that "more than 80 percent of Chinese families use Chinese Farmer's Almanac to find the lucky date and time for the special occasions like wedding, engagement, store grand opening, residential relocation and so on."

Also keep in mind, sources are not always from the printed word. Talk to people who actually plant and sow by the Moon phases. They can be your unique, in-the-flesh almanac of information. Sometimes older information is better: look to old newspaper or magazine articles you might find or the advice of older people who may have priceless information folded up in their containers of helpful gardening hints and tips from days gone by.

Compare and contrast your sources and try out different methods. Keep a journal to see what works best for you so that you can try it again or vary from your previous course!

New Moon

Gravity pulls toward the Moon and heaves water up. This can cause seeds to expand and break open. A full Moon also offers more light, encouraging stable root and leaf growth. This is an ideal time to plant crops that grow above the ground, like celery, cabbage, lettuce, and cauliflower.

Full Moon Phase from Waxing to Full Moon

When the Moon is half-illuminated and on its way to a full Moon, the pull of gravity is less than a full Moon, but the moonlight is still intense enough for strong leaf growth. This is a very good time to plant crops that produce above the ground but keep their seeds inside. Peppers, peas, melons, and tomatoes are good examples. If you can plant these two days before the full Moon, that's even better.

Waning Moon

Directly after the full Moon, the lunar energy draws down. The gravitational pull is powerful. This gives the soil moisture, making for a good time to plant root crops like carrots, onions, beets, and potatoes.

Herbs As Part of a Lunar Life

One way of connecting to nature and the phases of the Moon is to do a little lunar herbal gardening for your culinary delights. Planting and growing herbs has been a lifetime practice for some people. For others, going to the vegetable section or spice section of the grocery store has been their lifetime practice.

Select a Plant to Grow

First, of course, you want to decide want kind of herbs you want to grow based on what you will use them for.

Cooking Herbs

Some popular cooking herbs are basil, rosemary, thyme, parsley, and cilantro.

Aloe Vera

If you are using herbs for other reasons, such as herbal remedies, you might consider cultivating something like aloe vera, which can be done inside. Almost all of us have heard of aloe vera and some of its many benefits. It is worth the time to grow!

Buy a small plant at a grocery or garden shop and transplant it into a larger container, as it will have offshoots and needs a bit of space. Use a potting mix that's recommended for cacti and succulents and allows for good drainage. The plant will need full sun or it can thrive with artificial plant lights. Do the obvious when checking to see if it needs water. Stick your finger in the soil to test if it is dry. Be careful of the prickly leaves.

These plants usually only need to be watered every few days. Don't harvest the aloe gel from the plant until you need it.

When you split a leaf for the gel, the best way is to cut it off as close to the stem as possible. Use a knife or something you can wedge between the outer skin and the gel. This will cause the leaf to open and you can scoop out what you need. There are a lot of other complicated methods but this is a simple one.

When I am outside and need aloe for a bug bite, for example, I run to my closest aloe plant and just use my fingernail to split open the plant.

However, if you split open a leaf and have some to spare, it can stay in your refrigerator for up to a week in a plastic bag. If you have an interest in planting aloe, I suggest you look to some websites, such as www.wikihow.com/Grow-and-Use-Aloe-Vera-for-Medicinal-Purposes, or talk to a professional gardener about growing and utilizing this herbal plant.

Aloe is good for topical burn and bug bite applications and is known to aid in the healing of psoriasis. The medicinal aspects are plentiful, and it is always good to have on hand, especially in the kitchen. If a bit of grease flies out of my frying pan, I reach for the aloe vera, split a leaf, and pat the inner gel (although a bit slimy) on the burn. Aloe is an emollient and putting it on your skin can soften and hydrate it. It's basically a moisturizer that supplies oxygen to the skin cells. Got black and blue marks after that day of building your Moon altar or hanging that Moon phase poster that fell on your arm? Slap on some of this magical goo and watch the healing take place. Did you walk up that hill to see the lunar eclipse and now you have blisters? Apply a little aloe on them for relief. You can also drink aloe vera for digestive purposes, urinary tract infections, and other ailments.

However, if you decide to take it orally or juice it, speak to your doctor beforehand.

Select a Container

Growing plants in containers is an excellent choice for caring for and displaying your herb garden. That said, there is a little bit of controversy when it comes to herb containers.

- The **CERAMIC TERRA-COTTA POTS** would seem the way to go as they look so natural and that's what most people assume would work.
- Yet, many professional herb growers say **PLASTIC** is much better because clay pots can dry out and crack.

So if you like that terra-cotta look, you can get the plastic ones that resemble terra-cotta instead. I grow my own herbs, and although I am not a professional gardener by any means, I use the plastic and it works for me.

Any container will work as long as it is big enough to allow for root expansion and has plenty of drainage at the bottom. Although you want your herbs to look pretty, think of what is best for the plants. I saw someone plant herbs in antique tea cups, which looked beautiful, but there was no drainage except for a few rocks on the bottom, and the cups were way too small for the roots to grow properly. It made a great photo or display if you were selling a home, for example. But the poor little herbs didn't have a chance!

Growing Herbs Together

Sure, you can grow different herbs in one container, but they must be compatible.

Different herbs have different requirements. When planting herbs together, they need to require the same lighting, water, and fertilizer conditions. Plants can coexist in the same containers but do your research before you plant. For example:

- Rosemary enjoys soil that is drier and leaner (less fertilized). Basil likes more water and more fertilizer. So even if they respect each other, rosemary and basil can't live together in the same space.
- Sage, thyme, and rosemary have the same requirements (lots of sun and slightly dry soil), so they do well as a group.
- Mint has to be by itself. It can be invasive to other herbs and will grow rampant over them.

In addition to combining herbs that are well matched, some people add compatible flowers, such as pansies or marigolds, to their herbal containers to provide additional beauty. Ask your local garden center which plants and flowers will work well together if you're not sure.

Choosing Seeds or Plants

If you are planting your lunar herb garden from seeds, you will probably enjoy great satisfaction in seeing them sprout from near nothing to a full, lush herb. (We hope.) You can buy seeds online or in hardware stores and garden centers.

If you are buying started herbs, you are actually transplanting them. However, there is still a time for transplanting (within seven days of the full Moon, to be precise) which we will talk about it in the "Planting by the Phases of the Moon" section.

Personally, I buy the plants that are already started. I have tried the seeds as well, but I do better with the plants that can wave to me as I make my selection. Try both if you have the time and inclination.

Learn from my mistakes: always opt for healthy plants. I know your heart may go out to the little plant that has hardly any leaves and looks sickly. I know some of you probably think like I did, "Don't they water these herbs? I will save these from the garden center with no soul." Wrong! A sickly plant has to be quarantined from other herbs, as you can't always tell what's wrong with it at first. It could have bugs or the damage is already so severe that there is no saving it. Send it your blessing and let it go to plant heaven and move on. Always buy the healthiest and hardiest plant you can find. The healthy ones need homes too.

Find Quality Soil

All gardeners believe in starting anything in "good soil." But when you are dealing with herbs that go in containers, you actually want something that is labeled "potting mix"—NOT "potting soil." Potting soil can tend to be of a poor quality and clog the pot so drainage is not ideal. Potting mix is more organic and actually intended for plants in containers because it provides better drainage. Keep in mind that if you are using seeds, you will not see growth for a few weeks. But once they sprout, they will thrive.

Planting Seeds

1. Fill your container (that has good drainage, as we discussed earlier) with potting mix. Make sure there are no air pockets by patting down the soil, or else your seeds may drop too far down to the bottom of the pot.
2. This is an interesting method: For those who lean toward the very technical, you should plant your herb seeds about three times deeper than the seed itself. So, for example if the seed is a quarter inch, you

push it in three-quarters of an inch. Nevertheless, since seeds are so small, many people basically just push them into the soil about a quarter from the top.

Keep them in a sunny location that is warm.

Watering

Once you've planted your seeds, water them without flooding the pot. After that, you can go one of two routes:

1. Cover the container with plastic wrap. This allows the soil to stay warm, and you don't have to keep watering. In fact, with this method you don't have to water again until you see the seeds sprouting. (The seeds will eventually sprout and come into view.)
2. If you don't mind watering, skip the plastic wrap. This means you will have to water frequently. To check if the seeds need water, simply stick you finger into the soil. If it's dry an inch below the surface…water.

Herbs don't really need that much water, but when you do water, try to water in the morning hours if possible. This will allow the moisture to soak in without too much evaporation. Do not water over the leaves. Stick to watering around the stalk or shoot. Watering the leaves can encourage mildew and other diseases.

To Fertilize or Not to Fertilize

When you water your herbs, it washes away the nutrients from the potting mix, so you should use some type of fertilizer. There are many different kinds, but here are the two most popular options for lunar planters:

- If you make your own compost, that will work.
- A weak solution of fish emulsion about every two weeks is favored by lunar planters. You can buy it online or at most garden centers.

Add the fertilizer at the time of planting and every two to three weeks after that. Herbs don't need that much fertilizer. Excessive amounts can promote a lot of leaf growth but you won't have that concentrated flavor.

Where to Keep Your Herbs Inside

The best place is where they will get sun. If you are growing herbs for cooking, you probably want them in your kitchen where you can pluck a few sprigs or cut them to enhance one of your recipes. (By the way, herbs are resilient, so you really can just pluck pieces off.)

However, if your kitchen windowsill doesn't get sun and there isn't anywhere else in the kitchen that gets sun, you'll have to move them some other place. If you have a patio and want them outdoors, you can put them there or on a balcony—even on the back-porch steps. Or you may have to select the dining room or bedroom window. If you get little sun anywhere in your home, there are grow lights you can buy to induce growing.

The majority of herbs need about eight hours of sun. This is why you must research your choices before you buy. The best place for indoor herbs would be a windowsill that faces south, as this will be the warmest.

Now that you have your herbs picked out, you just need to look to the Moon's phases and determine which are ideal for your precious plants.

Planting by the Phases of the Moon

Thousands of years of gardening practice support planting herbs according to lunar phases. Proponents of lunar gardening report increased seed germination speed and success rates, along with enhanced overall plant health and quality. It's believed to be a combination of the Moon's gravitational, magnetic, and light forces that affect seed germination (planting), root growth (transplanting), and leaf growth. Whether you are growing from seeds or planting herbs that are already started, that lunar magic makes a difference. I have seen people grow herbs whenever the urge strikes them and those, like myself, who plant by the Moon. The Moon planters always had better-looking plants and, might I add, more flavorful herbs. Try it yourself!

- During the dark time of the **NEW MOON**, when the Moon exerts a strong gravitational pull on the earth, oceans tides rise. Similarly, the groundwater level beneath the soil is elevated. This allows seeds and roots to access and absorb water, fueling a rapid growth spurt, and aiding plants in setting down strong roots to support the next stage of growth. This is important for anything you're growing directly in the ground.
- Throughout the second week of the lunar cycle, as the Moon is **WAXING** and becomes full, leaf growth is accelerated due to extra exposure to light—specifically, the light of the Moon.
- At the **FULL MOON**, gravitational pull once again strengthens and plant roots experience another growth spurt while leaf growth remains relatively still.
- As the Moon begins to **WANE** and slowly darken over the third and fourth weeks of the lunar cycle, gravitational pull falls away as well. Plants experience a time of balance and rest, where the rate of growth slows in both roots and leaves. Then a new lunar cycle begins again.

Seed Germination Classifications

Because seeds germinate at different rates, lunar gardening methods can aid in optimizing germination and transplanting success. Seed germination is classified into three groups:

1. Short-germinating (SG) seeds (1–7 days)
2. Long-germinating (LG) seeds (8–21 days)
3. Extra-long-germinating (ELG) seeds (22+ days)

To increase the speed and success rate of seed germination:

- **PLANT SG AND ELG SEEDS WITHIN 7 DAYS OF THE NEW MOON.** It's best to germinate leafy, above-ground producing annuals, such as cilantro, during the increasing (waxing) phase. At the new Moon, when the lunar gravitational pull is at a high point, SG seeds quickly absorb water, which forces the seed coat to burst open, triggering a rapid growth spurt. For ELG seeds such as thyme, parsley, and rosemary, this time is used to absorb water and humic acid in preparation for germination during the next new Moon phase.
- **PLANT LG SEEDS WITHIN 7 DAYS OF THE FULL MOON.** The full Moon is the best time to plant LG seeds such as basil and dill. As moonlight and gravitational pull decrease following the full Moon and water levels in soil recede, LG seeds ready themselves for germination during the next new Moon phase. This waning Moon phase is also the best time to transplant seedlings into the outside garden and a good time to fertilize mature plants.

Pruning by Moon Phases

The best time to prune herbs is when the Moon is waning from half full until there's a dark Moon (when there is no visible sign of the Moon). This is a time to release and let go of those dead leaves and cut off old stems.

Making Your Own Infused Oils

We don't only cook with herbs—in fact, we can use them for other purposes. One popular option is making infused oils by adding the fragrance and taste of an herb to a simple "carrier oil," such as jojoba or almond oil. There are many other types of oils you can infuse with your own herbs. Here are a few suggestions:

- Mint can soothe muscle pain and headaches.
- Cayenne peppers can be used for soreness you may have on occasion.
- Thyme can be used for minor skin irritations.
- Lemon balm cools, calms, and relaxes the skin.

Who knows, it could be your new lunar hobby!

Other Uses for Popular Herbs

Many herbs have been used as natural remedies and spiritual symbols for centuries. Let your lunar herbal garden nourish you *and* heal you!

Basil

- Leave it to those passionate Italians to wear a spring of basil to indicate their future marriage.
- Got a headache? Try drinking tomato juice blended with fresh basil.
- In India, basil is considered sacred. It is esteemed largely for its medicinal properties. Harvesting or gathering basil is said to "awaken the senses and nourish your spirit."

Garlic

Many used to believe garlic gave you strength and courage. It's also been widely used against evil and dark forces. Must be the smell warding off these entities, but it does taste good.

Sage

- No toothbrush? No worries. American Indians used sage as a tooth cleaner.

- Sage is also used for smudging a space to purify it. The quick version of smudging is to light a small bundle of sage and allow it to flame for a moment. They actually sell sage bundles wrapped with rope or a string for this purpose. You can make your own, of course, by drying out the stems and bundling them together. Then you light the bundle and quickly blow out the flame. You now have a smoking bundle that you can more or less wave over an area or room like a wand, either in a back and forth or circular motion. This is said to remove negative energy from a location. Some people put sage in a fireproof bowl or seashell and do the same. Many people smudge a new house or apartment they are moving into. Did your ex just move out? Give it a smudge! Always be cautious when using anything that involves fire or sparks.

Tarragon

- Have a toothache? The ancient Greeks had a cure. They chewed tarragon because of its ability to numb the mouth.

• • •

Having an herbal lunar garden is a way of tapping into your creative side to produce something useful (and edible). There's nothing quite like having fresh herbs to cook with or to throw into a summertime libation. You'll feel like a pioneer of sorts, and there's nothing easier to grow! You don't have to have a green thumb to be successful with these tiny plants—just an understanding of the phases of the Moon. Plant wisely and watch your garden sprout!

CHAPTER 20
LUNAR MEAL RECIPES

Eating Moon-Inspired Foods

No matter what phase of the Moon we are in, we have to eat. The recipes I present to you in this chapter are compliments of some home chefs with great culinary skills and a love for the Moon. These Moon-driven foods are inspired by places near and far away that have traditions attached to lunar cuisine, events, and celebrations.

Moon Cakes

According to classic Confucian texts from around 500 B.C., ancient Chinese people held festivals to celebrate and honor the rebirth of the Sun in spring and the Harvest Moon in autumn. One of the early festival customs involved offering sacrifices to the Moon Goddess so that she would yield a plentiful harvest the following year. Hence, elaborate meals were prepared and laid out, with much of the food offered to deities of Chinese legends—and Moon cakes were one of the offerings, of course.

The most famous story surrounding the tradition of gifting Moon cakes to family and friends is a tricky one and doesn't involve the Moon Goddess at all, but rather the rebellion that succeeded in overthrowing the Mongol dynasty. As the story goes, a rebel leader gained permission to distribute thousands of Moon cakes to Chinese residents in the Mongol capital as a blessing to the longevity of the Mongol emperor. Baked inside each cake was a hidden message that read, "Uprising on the fifteenth day of the eighth month." Since the oppressive Mongols didn't eat Moon cakes, the secret plot went undiscovered until it was too late! Even though this legend is widely retold, there's not enough historic evidence to determine whether it's true. But some culinary historians view the secret message hidden in the Moon cakes to be the forerunner of the modern-day fortune cookie.

The Moon cake itself is a rich, indulgent treat that tends to be a delicate balance of sweet and savory, plus a variety of textures. Meant to be shared, customarily each cake is sliced into eight pieces, as the number eight is a favorable number for the Chinese.

Very few people who honor this tradition actually make the Moon cake themselves. They buy them because of the complexity of the recipe (which includes, of all things, lye water). So there you have it—this is one dish for which the legend is more important than the recipe!

Grilled Black and Blue Moon Burgers

If you are a moonstruck meat lover, I've got a terrific recipe for you! Although there are many ways to prepare a burger, this is a burger that you will want to cook more than just once in a black or blue Moon. Black and blue Moons are unique and always have a hint of mystery and magic to them. If you remember earlier, I said that the blue Moon is the extra or second full Moon within a month and that this phenomenon occurs approximately every two or three years. The black Moon is the dark twin to the blue Moon and is the third new Moon in a season of four new Moons. So what could be better than to combine these two unlikely twins into one meal at your next Moon phase cookout? *(Recipe developed by home chef Chris Shake.)*

SERVES 4

2 pounds 80/20 ground beef (containing 20% fat)
¼ cup blackened seasoning of your choice
8 ounces crumbled blue cheese
¼ cup butter or butter substitute
4 hamburger buns
Lettuce and tomatoes, optional, for toppings

1. Preheat outdoor grill or grill pan on the stovetop to medium-high.
2. Form 8 quarter-pound patties. Put a small indent in 4 of the patties.
3. Fill each cavity with 1 ounce blue cheese.
4. Cover each patty with other 4 remaining patties. Pinch and seal outside edges of burgers. Season both sides of patties with blackened seasoning.
5. Cut buns in half and butter both sides.

6. Grill burgers until desired doneness, approximately 4 minutes each side for medium. Cheese will be oozing out. Do not try to flatten them by pressing down with a spatula.
7. Put buns facedown on grill and lightly toast a few seconds.
8. Put burgers on buns and add 1 ounce leftover cheese to each patty. Add any condiments or toppings you like, such as lettuce and tomatoes.

Harvest Moon Spicy Rib Eye Stew

If you are looking for a hearty meal for your Harvest Moon Festival at home, try this savory dish. The Harvest Moon in September allowed farmers additional time to harvest their crops after the Sun had set. At this time, produce is bountiful—and so is this recipe, not only ingredient-wise but taste-wise too. Build your meal around the bounty—a true honor to this full Moon. It's also another way to spice up the night and impress your lunar diners. Make it a tradition! *(Recipe developed by home chef David Stahl.)*

SERVES 4

3 rib eye steaks, approximately 12 ounces each
1 onion, chopped
1 small (6-ounce) can tomato paste
8 poblano or ancho chilies
1 (16-ounce) can beef broth
5–6 large tomatoes
2 tablespoons olive oil, divided (approximate)
Salt and ground black pepper, to taste
4–5 large cloves fresh garlic
1 teaspoon garlic powder
1 tablespoon chili powder
1–2 teaspoons chili flakes
2 teaspoons rosemary
1 teaspoon thyme
1 tablespoon cumin

1. Roast (or broil) the poblano chilies at 400°F until the sides are black on all sides, approximately 5 minutes. Watch them closely. Remove and cool them; peel off blackened membrane and discard. Slice into strips. (Keep in mind

that the seeds are very spicy, but reserve some for the dish if you'd like to use them!)

2. Cut tomatoes in half, sprinkle with 1 tablespoon olive oil, salt, and pepper, and broil in a glass baking sheet at 400°F until tomatoes have a bit of char on the edges, approximately 5–8 minutes. Watch them carefully. (The oil and juice that runs out will go in the pot.)
3. In large pot, heat 1 tablespoon olive oil over high heat. Fry steaks until browned on each side.
4. Remove steaks to a separate dish to cool and then cut them into quarters. (The aim is to turn the bottom of the pot brown with caramelized juice from the meat.)
5. Deglaze pot first with onion until it's translucent and brown.
6. Stir in paste and add broth, mixing well.
7. Return meat to pot.
8. Add tomato halves and juices to pot.
9. Add chilies and reserved seeds. (Throw away the large cluster of seeds at the base of each stem or else it may be too spicy.)
10. Bring mixture up to a very low simmer and stir in garlic and spices.
11. Remove pot from heat, cover, and let rest for an hour or more.

Luna Tuna

With all this talk about how the Moon affects the tides, it's natural to look to a fish dish to celebrate the Moon. It's undemanding and inspired by the benefits we are gifted from that big sphere in the night! Curry powder, orange juice, and apricot jam add great flavor to tender tuna steaks. Because the steaks are simmered in the sauce, they pick up more flavor. *(Recipe developed by Susan Whetzel.)*

SERVES 4

2 tablespoons olive oil
1 onion, chopped
2 teaspoons curry powder
⅓ cup frozen orange juice concentrate
2 tablespoons water
¼ cup apricot jam
Salt and ground black pepper, to taste
4 (6-ounce) tuna steaks

1. In heavy skillet, heat olive oil over medium heat. Add onion; cook and stir for 2 minutes. Sprinkle curry powder over onions; cook and stir for 2–3 minutes longer, until onions are crisp and tender.
2. Add orange juice concentrate and water to skillet, along with apricot jam and salt and pepper. Bring to a boil; then reduce heat to a simmer and add tuna. Cook for 8–10 minutes per inch of thickness, turning tuna once during cooking time, until fish flakes when tested with fork. You can serve tuna medium-rare if you like.
3. Place tuna on serving plate. If necessary, reduce sauce by turning heat to high and simmering until thickened, 3–4 minutes. Pour sauce over tuna and serve.

Crème de Moon Cake with Mint

If you are watching your calories but crave something sweet now and then, try to put off indulging till a waning or dark Moon. Those phases are the time dieting is the easiest. As the Moon wanes, it releases things we don't want in life—and that, for many of us, would be calories. So I think it is fair to say to fellow Moon worshippers, if you have to pick a time to indulge in sweet treats, this is the phase. Therefore, I have included my friend and fellow moongazer Janet Osterholt's easy dessert. It's basically a box mix with a twist. For those of my moongazers who want to heat up their kitchen but don't want to quit their day jobs, this is a fun and simple recipe. No one will know you didn't spend hours on this. *(Recipe developed by home chef Janet Osterholt.)*

SERVES 8

1 box white cake mix
⅔ cup water (the box directions might say 1 cup, but use ⅔)
⅓ cup plus 3 tablespoons crème de menthe liquor, divided (contains alcohol)
1 (12.8-ounce) jar hot fudge topping (Hershey's is a good choice)
8 ounces frozen whipped topping, thawed (such as Cool Whip)

1. Prepare cake mix according to package directions, with one exception: use ⅔ cup water and ⅓ cup crème de menthe instead of 1 cup water. Put in 9" × 13" baking pan greased with nonstick spray.
2. While cake is warm (wait at least 5 minutes), spread hot fudge topping over cake while it's still in the pan. Refrigerate.
3. In medium bowl, combine remaining crème de menthe and whipped topping, mixing well.
4. Ice chilled cake with flavored whipped topping and serve.

Summer Solstice Shrimp Salad

The Summer Solstice is the beginning of summer and a time for renewal, The days are longer, and it gives us more time to reflect and enjoy the warmth of the season. A time for celebrations, outdoor activities, and staying cool. Hence, why not have a light meal at this time, like fresh shrimp, to cool you and your skywatcher friends? Try some Summer Solstice Shrimp Salad. Better yet, try to say that three times fast. But it's not the title, it's the taste. Even though we love the Sun, our focus is on our old lunar buddy. A way of remembering her is to find something that reminds you of her when you're preoccupied with the Sun. In that regard, shrimp is ideal. They do look like waxing Moons, yes? *(Recipe developed by home chef David Stahl.)*

SERVES 4

2 pounds fresh shrimp, steamed and peeled
2 cups chopped fresh cilantro (This is where that lunar herbal garden comes in handy.)
2 cups chopped spring onions
1 cup chopped sweet onion
2–3 hardboiled eggs, chopped
½ cup real mayonnaise
1 cup coleslaw (store-bought is fine unless you make your own)
¼ cup Ken's Sweet Vidalia Onion dressing
1 teaspoon garlic powder
1 teaspoon paprika
1 teaspoon cumin
Salt and ground black pepper, to taste

1. There are many methods for steaming shrimp, but the important aspect of all of them is that the shrimp are not in the water—so elevate them using a mesh strainer or steamer basket if you have one. The water should be at a

rapid boil. Cover and steam for 5–6 minutes until cooked through. Take them out after approximately 3 minutes and give them a toss to check that they are cooking evenly. They should have a pink look.

2. Mix all ingredients together in mixing bowl.
3. Chill. (Not you; I mean put the shrimp in the fridge.)

Cosmic Moon Latkes

Latkes (potato pancakes) are a traditional Hanukkah food. The Jewish tradition has many connections to the Moon. In fact, the new Moon is the start of every Jewish month. So not only do Jews look to the Moon for inspiration and direction, but in my opinion, they also make the best latkes. These delicious potato pancakes are a perfect accompaniment to breakfast, lunch, or dinner but are filling enough to eat on their own. Season them as desired; try them plain or topped with applesauce, ketchup, or even sour cream. Whether you like them sweet or savory—or just the way they are—you'll find yourself making them again and again.

SERVES 6

6 medium golden potatoes, peeled and grated
1 small onion, peeled and grated
2 large eggs, beaten
2 tablespoons unbleached all-purpose flour
1 tablespoon white whole-wheat flour
½ teaspoon freshly ground black pepper
¼ teaspoon ground nutmeg
1 cup peanut oil

1. Place potato and onion in a large mixing bowl. Add eggs, flours, pepper, and nutmeg and stir well to combine.
2. Heat oil in a large skillet over medium-high heat. Add ⅓ cup potato mixture to hot oil, flatten slightly with a spatula, and cook until golden brown and crisp on bottom, about 3–5 minutes. Flip gently and brown on second side another 3–5 minutes.
3. Remove from pan and drain on paper towels. Repeat process with remaining potato mixture.
4. Serve warm.

Vegetarian Dark Moon Tacos

When the Moon is waning to a dark Moon (getting smaller in size till you can see no Moon at all), many people believe in fasting for various reasons, ranging from health to spirituality. I know several people who practice a no-meat diet only for this phase, and it is a good time to do such. They do it as a form of a sacrifice to their higher power or just to cleanse their bodies from meat for a day.

SERVES 4

4 tortillas
1 cup black beans, rinsed, and drained
½ cup uncooked brown rice, prepared according to package directions
1 small onion, chopped into ¼" pieces
¼ cup whole-kernel corn
2 tablespoons freshly chopped cilantro
¼ cup canned green chilies or 2 fresh green chilies
¼ teaspoon salt
½ teaspoon ground black pepper
1 medium avocado, cut into ½" pieces
½ cup shredded Monterey jack cheese
½ cup salsa
½ cup shredded lettuce

1. Preheat oven to 350°F. Place tortillas in a covered ovensafe container and warm in the oven for 5–10 minutes.
2. Combine beans, rice, onion, corn, cilantro, chilies, salt, and pepper in a medium bowl. Mix well.
3. Remove tortillas from the oven and place ½ cup of rice-bean mixture in the center of each. Divide avocado, cheese, salsa, and lettuce evenly between tortillas.
4. Roll up each tortilla and fold over ends before serving.

Full Moon Breakfast

After a late night enjoying a full Moon, you'll be craving a hearty breakfast. The best thing is to prepare it the day before. This recipe can be made in advance, put in the fridge, and baked in the morning. Don't you love that? Trust me, you'll thank yourself. It's homemade, less expensive than eating out, and perfect for those of us who are too bleary-eyed in the morning to even think about cooking. Options include adding green peppers, onions, and jalapeños (lightly sautéed).

SERVES 4

7 large eggs, beaten
1 can (10.5-ounce) cream of mushroom soup
2 cups milk
1 pound pork breakfast sausage, cooked and crumbled
2 cups shredded Cheddar cheese
1 (16-ounce) package of croutons

1. Combine eggs, soup, and milk in a mixing bowl and mix well.
2. Grease a 9" × 13" baking dish.
3. Cover bottom of dish with croutons and sausage. Poor egg mixture on top of croutons and sausage. Top with cheese.
4. Cover and refrigerate overnight.
5. Before baking casserole, preheat oven to 350°F. Bake covered for 30 minutes.
6. Reduce heat to 325°F and continue baking uncovered 15 more minutes.

Houby (Mushroom) Soup

Some people like to go houby ("ho-bee") picking during a full Moon. *The Waterman and Hill-Traveller's Companion, a Natural Events Almanac* tells us the full Moon plays a large role in mushroom "flushes" (a period of time when large numbers of mushrooms appear all at once). What is a houby? It is a mushroom. The word is derived from the Czech and Slavic languages. There is even a Houby Festival in Berwyn and Cicero, Illinois, commemorating this mushroom hunting tradition. Mushrooms were a significant part of the Czech diet. Do always remember that if you are not an expert at identifying mushrooms, picking the wrong ones can be fatal. So opt for the grocery store and don't take chances. It's just so much safer. We don't know what Moon phase store-bought mushrooms were made in, but we can prepare them on a waxing or full Moon. The flavors abound and flourish!

SERVES: 8

1 pound white mushrooms
½ pound shiitake mushrooms, stems removed
1 teaspoon olive oil
4 sprigs fresh thyme or ½ teaspoon dried
4 or 5 shallots, peeled and chopped very fine
Pinch of salt plus more to taste
¼ cup dry white wine
2 cups vegetable stock or water
½ pound assorted wild mushrooms (chanterelle, shiitake, oyster, cremini, black trumpet, etc.) sliced into bite-sized pieces or an equal amount of sliced white mushrooms
2 teaspoons butter
Freshly ground black pepper to taste
3 cups cold milk
1 tablespoon finely chopped fresh chives

1. Pulse the white mushrooms in about four small batches in a food processor to finely chop them, stopping before they clump. Roughly hand-chop the shiitakes, then pulse them the same way.
2. Heat the oil in a 2½-cup saucepan over medium-high heat; toss in the thyme and allow to sizzle for a moment, then add the shallots and sauté 3 minutes until translucent. Add the chopped mushrooms. Sprinkle in a pinch of salt and cook 5–7 minutes until mushrooms are soft.
3. Add white wine and cook 2 minutes, then add the stock. Simmer 10 minutes.
4. Meanwhile, in a medium sauté pan over high heat, sauté the sliced mushrooms in the butter in small batches, seasoning them with salt and pepper as they cook. Set aside.
5. Put ⅓ of soup in blender with 1 cup cold milk and purée until very smooth. Repeat with remaining soup and milk, then season to taste. Be careful to vent the blender to avoid dangerous splashing. Serve with a spoonful of sautéed mushrooms in each bowl and a sprinkling of chives.

• • •

No matter what your appetite or your level of expertise in the kitchen, you can whip up one of these delicious delights without a whole lot of effort. Of course, whether you want to offer them up to the Moon Goddess or keep them for your friends and family (or your little old self) is up to you—but I think you're going to have a hard time not sneaking a bite or two. (Good thing the Moon Goddess is generous!)

CHAPTER 21

LUNAR BREWS AND CONCOCTIONS

Lunar Libations

Whether you are having a Moon phase party or just want a special beverage for yourself and a few good friends, here you will find some favorite lunar libations and mixtures to send you over the Moon.

"When the Moon is new…that sliver of light, I drink my tea to my delight
When the waxing Moon is growing near, then's the time for ginger beer
When the Moon is shrinking in the night, I look around for rum that's light
But when the Moon is full, like a big bright ball, that's the time I drink them all!"

—DIANE AHLQUIST

I have included cocktails with alcohol (starting with Moontini) and without alcohol (starting with Crescent Moon Mimic Champagne). A special note of thanks to my husband, Adrian, who not only created or enhanced most of the cocktails but also sacrificed to try them—all in the same day. What a guy!

Moontini

This recipe calls for vodka but you can also substitute gin, which was the classic potion. I am using vodka as it has evolved into America's favorite spirit since the '80s. Garnish with a cocktail onion. Those onions do resemble that luminous sphere in the sky, yes? Of course, if you prefer, you could use an olive. Which looks like an olive. Then again, maybe it looks like a lunar eclipse in green and red.

YIELDS 1 SERVING

2 parts vodka
⅓ part dry vermouth
1–2 cocktail onions

1. Fill mixing glass or shaker with ice cubes.
2. Add all the ingredients. Adjust the ratio to your own personal taste.
3. Shake and strain into a cocktail glass. Option: stir and shake. Try them both next to each other to see the difference, but don't get lune-y about it!

Moona Colada

Not all astral drinks have to be evening potions. A Moona Colada is a good daytime remedy for the heat and the summer Sun. And of course a coconut looks like a full Moon—a bit hairy, but full. A pineapple slice cut in half has the crescent Moon vibe, and the rum is what makes the cow jump over the Moon. How perfect is that?

YIELDS 4 SERVINGS

1 cup coconut milk
1 cup fresh pineapple juice (or as fresh as you can find)
½ cup good-quality rum, like Mount Gay for example
4 tablespoons light brown sugar
8 ice cubes
Pineapple slice (fresh or canned) for garnish

1. Put all ingredients except pineapple slice into a blender and blend until smooth.
2. Cut pineapple slice in half to form a crescent.
3. Serve in your favorite tropical glasses. Garnish rims with pineapple crescents. Don't forget the tiny umbrella in case of a lunar shower!

Lunar Punch for the Full Moon Bunch

Having a full Moon ceremony? Put a little punch into it! It's always fun to have different recipes like this for a unique addition to the celebration. Try using a vintage punch bowl with matching cups. You can find them at thrift stores, online, or even new with that vintage "look." Don't want to use a punch bowl? Use a big old pot, like a lobster pot or Dutch oven, to mix your brew. Add a ladle and a few glasses, and you're good to go. Since we all know the Moon is made of cheese, have a tray of various cheeses to serve with it so there is not too much lunacy on an empty stomach. Enjoy!

YIELDS 6 (6-OUNCE) SERVINGS

6 ounces pineapple juice
6 ounces guava juice
6 ounces pulp-free orange juice
6 ounces quality ginger ale
6 ounces ginger beer (homemade or store-bought; a homemade recipe appears later in this chapter)
6 ounces high-quality dark rum, like Mount Gay or Myer's
5 drops or shakes of Angostura bitters
Lime or any fruit you prefer for garnish

1. Add all ingredients to your punch bowl or pitcher. Stir, stir, stir and serve, serve, serve.
2. Float some lime around on top if using a punch bowl. If you are using a punch bowl, fill your glasses with ice instead of letting the ice melt in the bowl and dilute your drink!

Moony Mary

Remember in Chapter 16 when I talked about how the Moon will appear varying shades of red when there is a higher quantity of dust particles in the atmosphere? Well, what better time to enjoy a tomato juice-based concoction? Don't want the vodka? Remove it and make a Virgin Moony Mary.

YIELDS 6 SERVINGS

3 cups bottled Bloody Mary mix, like Mr. and Mrs. T's (Yes, the easy way out is okay.)
1 teaspoon freshly chopped dill (Get it from your lunar garden, if you have one.)
1 teaspoon hot pepper sauce
2 tablespoons dill pickle juice
5 tablespoons Old Bay Seasoning
1 fresh lime, squeezed
6 ounces vodka
6 pickle spears
1 fresh lime, cut into crescent moon slices

1. In a pitcher or container that will hold all the ingredients, mix together the Bloody Mary mix, dill, hot pepper sauce, and pickle juice. Adjust ratios according to taste.
2. Squeeze lime juice on a plate or saucer.
3. Put Old Bay Seasoning on a plate. You might have to add more later, depending on how much you use.
4. Dip individual glasses into lime juice to coat the rim.
5. Then press glass rim into Old Bay Seasoning.
6. Fill each glass with ice. Pour 1 ounce shot of vodka into each glass.
7. Fill glasses with the Moony Mary mix you have created and garnish with lime crescents and pickle spears.

Moony Mary for the Lazy Loner

Sometimes you just may want to be alone with your favorite Moon phase and just be. And typically, when someone wants to "just be," they are not too keen on doing a lot of prep work on meals or drinks. That's where this libation comes in. Less mixing and more time to gain lunar wisdom.

YIELDS 1 SERVING

1 cup Mr. and Mrs. T's Bloody Mary mix
1 ounce vodka
½ teaspoon horseradish
1 celery stalk

1. Pour Bloody Mary mix into a tall glass.
2. Add vodka and horseradish.
3. Mix with celery stick and leave celery in glass as garnish.

Moon Glow Shandy

This shandy is not only for once in a blue Moon—it might become your favorite cocktail. Try both versions and compare. It's the perfect party drink for those who want only a hint of a spirited blend. If you are looking for a libation with just a bit of spirits, this is a good choice. In fact, I have provided two versions so you can customize it to your tastes and tolerance levels!

Method One—with Beer:

YIELDS 2 (8-OUNCE) SERVINGS

8 ounces chilled beer (light or regular)
8 ounces chilled ginger ale
Two lime wedges

Evenly divide beer and ginger ale between 2 glasses. Stir. Add lime wedge to each glass.

Method Two—with Wine

YIELDS 2 (8-OUNCE) SERVINGS

8 ounces chilled chardonnay or white wine
8 ounces chilled ginger ale or store-bought guava pineapple juice (Welch's makes a good one.)
Two lime wedges

Evenly divide wine and ginger ale between 2 glasses. Stir and add lime wedge to each. Depending on taste, you can always adjust the ingredient ratios.

Moon over Margarita

This tequila drink can leave you bewitched and bewildered. So be cautious, or you will be looking at your lunar vision board for two days with your eyes crossed.

YIELDS 1 LARGE SERVING

2 ounces tequila
1 ounce triple sec
1 ounce pulp-free orange juice
⅓ ounce plus more for dipping fresh lime juice
1 tablespoon kosher or margarita salt
Lime or orange wedge for garnish

1. Use a cocktail shaker full of ice or improvise if you don't have one.
2. Add tequila, triple sec, orange juice, and lime juice to shaker.
3. Dip rim of glass into lime juice, then dip in salt to cover the rim.
4. Shake and strain over rimmed glass.
5. Garnish with a lime or orange wedge.
6. If you want it frozen, combine tequila, triple sec, and juices in a blender with plenty of ice.

Moon Magic Mint Mojito

While planting your new lunar herbs or just admiring the ones you already have, pull a few sprigs from your mint plant to conjure up a drink that would make the Moon Goddess smile. Or, you can have friends over and make those plans for that full Moon ceremony. The plans sometimes can be much more creative after a Moon Magic Mint Mojito or two. (Make sure no one's driving!)

YIELDS 1 (10-OUNCE) SERVING

10 fresh mint leaves, plus a few for garnish (from your garden or store-bought)
1 lime, sliced
2 tablespoons white sugar
1½ ounces white rum
1 cup ice cubes
½ cup club soda

1. Add mint leave to a tall glass.
2. Add 1 lime slice.
3. Crush mint and lime to release mint oils and lime juice. People use what is called a "muddler," which is like a long pestle, to mash the mint and lime. If you don't have one, you can improvise and use the back of a spoon or anything else that will mash.
4. Add 2 additional lime slices and sugar. Crush again.
5. Fill glass with ice, but not completely to the top.
6. Pour rum over ice. Fill rest of the glass with club soda.
7. Stir and taste. (Add more sugar if you'd like.)
8. Garnish with mint leaves and a full Moon lime slice. (Full lime slice cut with a small slit to perch on to the edge of the glass.)

Crescent Moon Mimic Champagne

Champagne has been the traditional drink of celebrations and festivities for the last 425 years. Even if you don't like it, everybody knows about it. So why not toast to the next Moon phase as it starts its journey through the month?

YIELDS 1 (5-OUNCE) SERVING

1 ounce chilled peach nectar
4 ounces chilled lemon-lime soda

1. Simply get a champagne flute, or you can use the old-fashioned kind (which is called a "coupe"—those are the kind that legends like Marilyn Monroe drank from in old-time movies).
2. Pour nectar into glass and add soda.
3. Gently stir and serve.

Punch with Full Moon Ice Ring

If you're having one or two people over for a Moon Festival, you may as well have fourteen. It's usually still the same amount of work. And do give the guests a bit of cheese and fruit. If you are ambitious, prepare cheese cubes in the shape of a Moon phase. Just cutting them in a big round circle works too.

YIELDS APPROXIMATELY 14 (6-OUNCE) SERVINGS

Ingredients for punch:

4 cups club soda
1 liter ginger ale (buy high-quality ginger ale...there is a difference)
3 cups unsweetened white grape juice

Ingredients for ice ring:

2 liters ginger ale
Fruit for ice ring, such as raspberries or canteloupe

1. Chill club soda, ginger ale, and grape juice at least overnight. Blend club soda, 1 liter ginger ale, and grape juice together.
2. To make the ice ring, fill a ring-shaped Bundt cake pan with 1 liter ginger ale.
3. Partially freeze, then add crescent-shaped fruit around the ring. Fill Bundt pan with remainder of ginger ale and freeze until it is as solid as a full Moon.
4. Place your full Moon ice ring in the punch bowl before serving.

Wassail Moon Drink

Wassailing dates way back to when farmers living in apple-growing regions of England would shout while pouring cider on their trees to keep evil spirits at a distance. With all that wassailing, a healthy crop was assured for the coming harvest. The cider transformed into many different concoctions through the years. It is thought that it originated from spice-sweetened wine with some type of honey into a hot punch-like brew. This nonalcoholic version soothes your soul as the winter Moon waxes and the full Moon is on the rise—or really anytime.

YIELDS 10 SERVINGS

2 quarts apple cider
1 cup pulp-free orange juice
1 cup pineapple juice
1 tablespoon light brown sugar
1 teaspoon lemon juice
2 cinnamon sticks
Dash ground cinnamon
Dash ground cloves

1. Bring all ingredients in a large saucepan to a boil. Reduce heat and cover.
2. Simmer for approximately 20 minutes. Remove and discard the cinnamon sticks.
3. Serve hot in mugs or cups. Also can be kept warm in a slow cooker.

Ginger Beer

This brew has no alcohol by nature and is best made during a waning Moon when the flavor of gingerroot releases more easily from this spicy herb. In spite of this, you can really make it anytime, but if you like to conduct experiments, try it during all the Moon phases and see if there is a difference. Keep a log of it! This particular recipe is contributed from a friend of mine, Angela, who hails from Barbados. That said, ginger beer is making a big splash these days. If you have never had authentic ginger beer, you don't know what you are missing. It is worth the effort. There is no comparison to the store-bought version. And store-bought versions certainly don't create Moon magic. The benefits of ginger beer are plentiful because the primary ingredient is gingerroot. It is said that gingerroot helps relieve nausea and possibly fight inflammation. It is also thought to soothe stomach-related issues. There are no guarantees, but the drink itself is very unusual. Most people who try it for the first time have to think about whether or not they like it. Usually, it's a thumbs up. If the ginger beer tastes too strong, you can dilute it with a little club soda or water. Do not keep the ginger beer for extended periods of time. It should be consumed within two days.

YIELDS 10 (6-OUNCE) SERVINGS

2 quarts water
1½ cups freshly minced ginger
2 whole lime peels (Only the lime peel, as any lime juice can change the taste of the ginger.)
¾ cup white sugar (Don't use brown sugar as it will change the color.)

1. Heat water over medium-low heat in a 4-quart sauce pan till warm (not boiling).

2. Blend together ginger and 2 cups of the warm water in a blender on medium speed. Add more water if needed.
3. Add ginger mixture, lime peels, and sugar to remaining warm water, stir until sugar is dissolved. Add more sugar to taste.
4. Cover and let stand overnight. Do not refrigerate at this point.
5. Strain the mixture through cheesecloth to remove the blended ginger. The drink should be clear and light in color.
6. Store in clean bottles or container in refrigerator.

Honeymoon/Summer Solstice Mead Drink

Before what we know as alcohol existed, the drink du jour was mead—a fermented honey and water mixture that sometimes had spices added with fruit and malt. The word *mead* comes from the Old English word for "meadow." When a couple first got married, they would drink mead for the first month of their wedlock. It was believed to have aphrodisiac properties. Hence, the word *honeymoon*. The June Moon is often called a Mead Moon. Depending on your taste, add cinnamon, nutmeg, or clove to make it a bit spicier. Or add some mint to give it a little kick!

YIELDS 21 (6-OUNCE) SERVINGS

2 cups apple juice
4 cups honey of your choice
6 cups filtered water or spring water
1 whole lemon, sliced (can use lime also)
1 whole orange, sliced

1. Using a large pot or saucepan that is nonmetallic, bring all the ingredients to a boil.
2. Reduce heat and simmer for about a half an hour. Use a wooden spoon to skim off any skin that starts to form on the top of mixture.
3. Let mixture cool, then strain it into some type of container and refrigerate.
4. Serve after it has cooled or chilled the next day.

CONCLUSION

Using the Moon to channel energy can make your life flow more easily. It's not all about the tides and water levels. There is an appeal to your subconscious mind via your lunar viewpoint. If you have faith in the idea there are things beyond the physical, use this book as a launchpad to an astral adventure. See for yourself which types of Moon magic you can incorporate into your life. Stay open to this gift of nature and all the enchantment and benefits the Moon can bestow upon you.

BIBLIOGRAPHY

Ahlquist, Diane. *Moon Spells* (Avon, MA: Adams Media, 2002).

Assaraf, John. *The Complete Vision Board Kit* (New York, NY: Atria Books, 2008).

Farmer's Almanac Calendar: Play Your Day. Grow Your Life (Ontario, Canada: Brown Trout Publishers Inc. Almanac Publishing Co., 2016).

Silbey, Uma. *The Complete Crystal Guidebook* (San Francisco, CA: U-Read Publications, 1986).

Website Resources

www.12soulsteps.com

www.allrecipes.com

www.astrology.com

Brett, Jennifer, N.D. "Aloe Vera: Herbal Remedies," http://health.howstuffworks.com/wellness/natural-medicine/herbal-remedies/aloe-vera-herbal-remedies.htm

Dugan, Ellen. "Easy Moon Gardening," http://llewellyn.com/journal/article/1893

Evans, Lisa. "6 Scents that Can Transform Your Mood and Productivity," www.entrepreneur.com/article/224575

www.farmersalmanac.com

www.growingandusingherbs.com

Macrae, Fiona. "Lunacy? Women are more fertile during a new moon and most likely to conceive during the darkest nights, say scientists," www.dailymail.co.uk/health/article-2807180/Women-fertile-new-moon-likely-conceive-darkest-nights-say-scientists.html.

National Aeronautics and Space Administration. "Earth's Moon," https://moon.nasa.gov/home.cfm

www.naturealmanac.com/archive/morels/mushrooms_moon.html

W. Atlee Burpee & Co. "Container Herbs," www.burpee.com/gardenadvicecenter/herbs/basil/container-herbs/article10008.html

www.wikihow.com/Grow-and-Use-Aloe-Vera-for-Medicinal-Purposes

Wikihow. "How to Determine Your Moon Sign," www.wikihow.com/Determine-Your-Moon-Sign

www.wikipedia.org

INDEX